The God Center

Dr Víctor Denis Purcell

Published by Dr Víctor Denis Purcell, 2024.

THE GOD CENTER

First edition. March 8, 2024.

Copyright © 2024 Dr Víctor Denis Purcell.

ISBN: 979-8224528417

Written by Dr Víctor Denis Purcell.

The God Center: The ultimate journey within.

"The God Center: The Ultimate Journey Inward" profoundly explores spiritual awakening and self-discovery. This book guides those seeking to delve into the mysteries of their existence and the universe. Each chapter is a step towards understanding the soul's journey.

Beginning with "The Awakening," the reader is introduced to the subtle stirrings of spiritual consciousness, exploring the initial signs of a more profound calling within the soul. This awakening leads to "The Seeker's Path," where the journey of questioning and yearning for truth begins, guiding the seeker towards understanding their place in the greater cosmos.

In "The Garden of Silence," meditation and finding peace in stillness are emphasized, creating a sanctuary within. "Echoes of the Ancient" connects readers with timeless wisdom and teachings, showing how ancient truths have guided humanity's spiritual quest.

"The Labyrinth of the Self" takes readers on a deep dive into self-reflection and introspection, challenging them to confront their inner complexities. "The Alchemy of Transformation" discusses the transformative power of spiritual experiences, turning base experiences into spiritual enlightenment.

"The Bridge of Connection" emphasizes connecting with others on the journey and exploring the spiritual bonds that unite us. "The River of Surrender" focuses on letting go and trusting in higher powers, while "The Light of Enlightenment" describes the moment of achieving spiritual clarity.

The book concludes with "The Return," where the journey comes full circle, and the seeker returns to the world with new wisdom, ready to live out the lessons learned.

"The God Center: The Ultimate Journey Inward" is not just a book; it's a companion for anyone on the path of spiritual exploration, offering insight, comfort, and guidance. It's a journey that promises to transform, enlighten, and connect the reader to the most profound truths of existence.

Chapters:

Introduction:

"The God Center: The Ultimate Journey Inward" explores the human spirit and its quest for more profound truth. This book is an invitation to journey into the deepest realms of self-awareness and spiritual consciousness. It guides us through a transformative path that enlightens and enriches our understanding of existence.

We begin this journey by acknowledging the inherent longing within each of us—a longing for meaning, purpose, and connection. This universal quest transcends cultural and societal boundaries, uniting us in our search for something greater than ourselves. Through these pages, we explore this profound longing, seeking to uncover the truths that lie at the very core of our being.

The God Center is not just a book but a companion on your journey toward self-discovery and spiritual enlightenment. As you turn each page, you will find yourself delving deeper into the mysteries of your existence. You will encounter questions that challenge your perceptions, stir your emotions, and awaken your soul. These questions are not merely rhetorical; they are the keys that unlock the doors to your innermost self.

In this journey, we embrace the idea that the inward journey is the most significant. The trip takes courage and openness, as it involves confronting our deepest fears, desires, and truths. Yet, it is also a journey filled with immense beauty and potential for growth. Each chapter in this book is a step on this path, offering guidance, insight, and wisdom to light the way.

We explore various aspects of the human experience—awakening, seeking, silence, ancient wisdom, self-reflection, transformation, connection, surrender, enlightenment, and return. Each of these themes is a vital component of the journey inward. They offer perspectives and insights that are both timeless and profoundly relevant to our modern lives.

As you engage with this book, you can approach it with an open heart and mind. Allow the words to resonate with your own experiences and reflections. This book is about reading, experiencing, feeling, and transforming. It is about discovering your own God Center, that sacred space within where true wisdom and peace reside.

This journey is as unique as each individual who embarks upon it. There is no single path to the truth, no one-size-fits-all approach to spiritual discovery. Therefore, this book offers a tapestry of insights, allowing you to find your way, guided by your inner wisdom and the universal truths that echo throughout these pages.

As you move through "The God Center: The Ultimate Journey Inward," embrace the journey with all its twists and turns. Let it be a transformative experience that leads you to a deeper understanding of yourself and your place in the universe. May this book serve as a beacon of light on your path, guiding you towards a deeper, more profound sense of being and a greater appreciation of the mystical journey of life.

Chapter 1

Whispers of the Soul, as the first subcategory of "The Awakening" in "The God Center: The Ultimate Journey Inward," speaks to the subtle yet profound early signs of spiritual awakening. It embodies the quiet, often unnoticed moments where our deeper consciousness starts to stir, signaling the beginning of a transformative journey.

In this initial phase, individuals may experience an unexplainable longing, a yearning for something more than the material world offers. This feeling often arrives without warning, during moments of quiet reflection or amidst the chaos of everyday life. It is a call from within, urging one to explore beyond the known and the visible, hinting at a more profound reality beneath everyday experiences.

Intuition begins to play a more significant role. People trust their gut feelings and inner voice more than they used to. This newfound reliance on inner guidance is a crucial indicator of the soul attempting to communicate, guiding one towards paths and decisions that resonate more deeply with one's true essence.

There's also an increased sensitivity to the beauty and mystery of the universe. Nature, art, and even simple everyday occurrences can take on a profound significance, imbuing one with a deeper meaning or connection to something larger than oneself. This heightened appreciation is like a whisper from the soul, affirming the interconnectedness of all things.

Many report feeling detached from material desires and ambitions that once seemed crucial. This detachment is not born out of disinterest or apathy but rather from a deepening understanding that true fulfillment comes from within. It's a subtle shift in perspective, focusing more on internal growth and less on external achievements.

Dreams may become more vivid or symbolic during this phase. They start to reflect the inner workings of the subconscious mind, often providing insights and guidance. In this context, dreams bridge the conscious and the subconscious, allowing wisdom to flow from the depths of the self.

Synchronicities – those meaningful coincidences that seem too apt to be mere chance – become more noticeable. These synchronicities are like nods from the universe, affirming that one is on the right path. They serve as encouragement to continue the inward journey, reassuring the seeker of their connection to a more fantastic plan.

There's a growing interest in spiritual or philosophical literature and discussions. Books, conversations, and even random encounters revolve around themes of spirituality, purpose, and the nature of existence. This intellectual curiosity manifests the soul's desire to understand and connect with something more significant.

An increasing sense of empathy and compassion towards others develops. This empathy directly results from the soul's awakening, as one begins to see themselves in others and understand the interconnectedness of all life. This compassion extends beyond human connections, encompassing all living beings and the environment.

Lastly, the emergence of a quiet, inner voice that offers guidance and reassurance becomes more prominent. This voice, distinct from the everyday mind's chatter, speaks with wisdom and clarity, guiding one towards choices and actions that align with one's true self. It's a sign that the soul is beginning to take a more active role in one's life, marking the beginning of a profound spiritual journey.

The exploration deepens into the nature of existence and our understanding of the world, marking the beginning of a profound inquiry into life's purpose and the mysteries of the universe.

The journey starts with an inner nudge, a feeling that there is more to life than what meets the eye. This sensation often surfaces in quiet moments of reflection or amid the routine of daily life. A gentle yet persistent question arises from within: Is there more to life than this? This question becomes the seed of a larger quest for deeper understanding and truth.

As this questioning deepens, one begins to look at the world with new eyes. Once taken for granted, the structures and beliefs feel less solid less absolute. There's a growing sense that the reality we perceive might be a small part of a much larger, more intricate tapestry of existence. This realization can be both exhilarating and unsettling.

In this search for deeper meaning, the conventional answers about life and success no longer seem sufficient. The societal benchmarks for happiness and achievement start to lose their allure, making way for a quest for something more authentic and profound. This shift in perspective is often the first step toward a significant personal transformation.

This questioning phase also brings a sense of solitude, as the journey is highly personal and unique to each individual. It can feel like one is treading a path that few others understand. Yet, this solitude is not about loneliness; it's about discovering a deeper connection with oneself and, ultimately, with the universe.

The more one questions, the more one realizes that many of life's most significant questions have no easy answers. This understanding leads to a sense of humility and openness to the mysteries of life. It becomes clear that not knowing is a part of the journey and that the quest for understanding is more about the journey than the destination.

Many find themselves drawn to various spiritual and philosophical traditions in this quest. These ancient wisdoms offer different perspectives and insights into the nature of reality and existence. They act as guides and maps, helping to navigate the unknown terrain.

This questioning also leads to a more profound appreciation for the present moment. As one begins to question the nature of reality, the beauty and richness of the current moment become more apparent. There's a realization that life is unfolding in complexity and mystery.

The process of questioning reality often leads to an expansion of consciousness. It opens up new realms of thought and perception, allowing one to experience life more fully and profoundly. This expanded consciousness becomes a gateway to deeper understanding and connection with the universe.

Finally, this journey of questioning is an ongoing process. It doesn't end with finding a definitive answer; instead, it's a continuous exploration that evolves and deepens over time. Each question leads to discoveries, new insights, and further questions, making life a rich and endless journey of discovery. This constant evolution of thought and understanding keeps the journey fresh and engaging, ensuring that the search for meaning and truth remains a vibrant and integral part of one's life.

In the realm of questioning reality, we find ourselves at the threshold of a profound awakening. Here, we begin to see beyond the veil of ordinary perception, sensing the deeper truths that lie just out of sight. This process is not merely an intellectual exercise but a soulful quest for understanding the very fabric of existence.

We listen to the whispers of the universe, beckoning us to look deeper into the nature of all that is. These whispers come in fleeting moments, urging us to question our long-held beliefs and the reality we've always known. It is a call to embark on a journey beyond the physical into the realms of the metaphysical.

The world around us transforms as we engage in this questioning. What once seemed solid and unchangeable now appears fluid and full of possibilities. We understand that reality is not a fixed entity but a dance of energy and consciousness, continuously unfolding in myriad forms.

We find ourselves drawn to the world's ancient wisdom, seeking guidance in the teachings of mystics and sages who have traversed this path before us. Their words, steeped in the mysteries of ages, offer us glimpses into the profound nature of our existence and the universe at large.

In this journey of questioning, we encounter the paradox of knowing and not knowing. We recognize the limits of our understanding, and this humbles us. Yet, in this space of not comprehending, the most incredible wisdom often reveals itself, like a star shining brightest on the darkest night.

We explore the interconnectedness of all life, sensing our oneness with the universe. This realization dawns upon us not as a concept but as a living, breathing truth. We see ourselves in the trees, the stars, the mountains, and the seas, understanding that we are all expressions of the same cosmic dance.

The beauty of the present moment becomes ever more apparent. We no longer live solely in the past or the future; instead, we find richness in the here and now. Each moment holds infinite possibilities, and we become keenly aware of life's miraculous unfolding.

Our dreams take on new dimensions, serving as portals to deeper realms of consciousness. They become our guides, offering symbols and messages that help us navigate the journey within. These nightly voyages are more than mere figments of our imagination; they are voyages into the depths of our souls.

We find that in questioning reality, we are also asking ourselves. Who are we beyond the labels and roles we've assumed? This inquiry leads us to discover our true nature, a being of light and infinite potential, temporarily clothed in the garb of human experience.

As we delve deeper into this journey of questioning, we realize that each question is a stepping stone to higher understanding. We embrace the mystery, knowing that the path of discovery is endless and that each step brings us closer to the divine essence within us all. This is not just a journey of the mind but an odyssey of the spirit, leading us to the heart of all that is.

In exploring "Signs and Synchronicities," we embark on a mystical journey where the universe communicates through subtle, often overlooked messages. These messages offer profound insights and guide us toward our true path when observed and understood.

We notice patterns and coincidences in our daily lives that defy ordinary explanations. These are not mere accidents but the language of the universe, speaking to us in a code that, once deciphered, reveals deeper meanings and connections. They are the universe's way of nodding in affirmation, signaling that we are in sync with the flow of life.

The more we attune ourselves to these signs, the more frequently they appear. Our awareness opens portals to a realm where time and space converge in meaningful alignments. These synchronicities are like breadcrumbs on our spiritual path, leading us to our next steps or affirming our current direction.

Dreams become a powerful medium for these messages. In our sleep, the mind's boundaries relax, allowing the subconscious to communicate through symbols and scenarios that, upon waking reflection, provide clarity and guidance. These dream messages often hold the key to understanding our deeper desires and fears, pointing us toward healing and growth.

Nature speaks to us in this language of signs and synchronicities. The fluttering of a butterfly, the pattern of leaves, and the ebb and flow of tides carry messages for those who know how to listen. Nature becomes a mirror, reflecting the inner workings of our soul.

In moments of stillness, we may hear the whisper of intuition, a subtle yet profound sense that guides our decisions and actions. This internal compass points us towards choices that align with our highest good, even when they defy logic or reason.

We find that our encounters with others are often not by chance but are arranged by the universe to teach us valuable lessons or to bring us the support and companionship we need. People enter our lives as bearers of wisdom, love, and challenges, each playing a role in our spiritual evolution.

Art and creativity become channels for these divine messages. A piece of music, a painting, a line in a poem - each can be a vessel carrying profound spiritual insights tailored to our journey. Art transcends the physical, touching the soul and speaking the language of the spirit.

The practice of meditation and mindfulness heightens our sensitivity to these signs. In the silence of our inner being, we become receptive to the subtle frequencies of the universe, tuning into the guidance that is always there, waiting to be acknowledged.

Finally, we realize that recognizing and interpreting these signs is a skill that develops over time. It requires patience, trust, and openness to the unknown. As we grow in this practice, the universe reveals its mysteries in ever more profound and beautiful ways, leading us closer to the ultimate truth of our existence.

In the mystical exploration of "Signs and Synchronicities," we discover a universe rich in communication, speaking to us through coincidences that are too precise and timely to be mere chance. These synchronicities are the universe's way of sending messages, guiding us on our spiritual path, and reassuring us that we are aligned with our true purpose.

Everyday life becomes a canvas for these signs, where ordinary moments are imbued with extraordinary messages. A chance encounter, a book falling open to a specific page, or overhearing a conversation that resonates deeply are not random occurrences but meaningful events orchestrated by the cosmos, guiding us subtly yet powerfully.

We learn to recognize these signs by tuning into our intuition, the silent voice within that understands the language of the universe. This inner knowing acts as a compass, pointing us towards choices and decisions that resonate with our soul's journey. Trusting this intuition becomes crucial in deciphering the messages hidden in plain sight.

Nature speaks to us in this mystical language of signs. A sudden gust of wind, the flight pattern of birds, the blooming of a flower at an unexpected time – all carry messages from the universe if we only know how to interpret them. These natural phenomena become symbols, reflecting insights about our inner world.

Our dreams become vivid landscapes of symbolic communication. In the dreamscape, our subconscious mind weaves intricate stories that, when reflected upon, offer guidance and clarity about our waking life. These dreams are a direct line to the more profound wisdom that resides within us.

Synchronicities often occur in times of need or transition, appearing as beacons of light guiding us through the darkness. They affirm that we are not alone in our journey and that a greater force guides and supports us. These moments remind us that our lives are interconnected with a larger, cosmic story.

Artistic expressions, whether in music, literature, or visual arts, often serve as vessels for these synchronistic messages. A line in a poem, a melody, or an image can strike a chord deep within us, resonating with our current situation or a question we've been pondering, providing insights and answers.

As we cultivate mindfulness, our awareness of these signs intensifies. We become more attuned to the subtle language of the universe, noticing synchronicities that we might have previously overlooked. This heightened awareness is a gateway to a deeper connection with the divine.

These signs and synchronicities often lead us to encounter people who play pivotal roles in our spiritual journey. These soulful connections are no accidents; they are divinely orchestrated meetings that bring growth, learning, and sometimes challenges, all serving our higher evolution.

Embracing this world of signs and synchronicities transforms our perception of reality. We begin to see life not as a series of random events but as a beautifully choreographed dance where every movement, every encounter, and every moment is significant. This perspective brings a sense of wonder and magic to our existence, revealing all things' interconnectedness and a deeper, mystical order at work.

In the mystical exploration of "Dreams and Visions," we delve into the realm where the subconscious mind speaks in symbols and narratives. This realm bridges the conscious world and the vast, uncharted territories of the spirit. Dreams become the canvas on which our deeper self paints messages, warnings, and wisdom.

The night brings a tapestry of dreams, each thread woven with the colors of our deepest fears, desires, and hopes. These dreams are not mere figments of imagination; they are revelations from the depths of our psyche, guiding us toward self-understanding and enlightenment. In their symbolism, we find keys to unlock the mysteries of our souls.

Visions, whether experienced in meditation or moments of heightened awareness, serve as powerful glimpses into the spiritual realm. They are windows that briefly show us possibilities, truths, and the deeper layers of reality usually hidden from our conscious minds. These visions are gifts, offering us guidance and insight.

Dreams often speak in a cryptic language, requiring interpretation and contemplation. A flying dream might symbolize freedom or escape; a dream of falling could reflect fears of losing control. As we learn to interpret these symbols, we gain access to a wellspring of wisdom within our subconscious.

In some traditions, dreams are seen as prophetic, offering predictions. Whether or not one believes in the predictive nature of dreams, it is undeniable that they often have a way of highlighting our most profound truths and guiding us toward our destiny.

Lucid dreaming, where one becomes aware they are dreaming and can exert control over the dream, becomes a practice of exploring the subconscious mind. It is a space where we can confront our fears, meet our shadow selves, and even practice skills or research solutions to waking life problems.

Dream journals become essential tools for those embarking on this journey. By recording and reflecting on our dreams, we develop a deeper understanding of the patterns, themes, and messages that our subconscious is communicating. This practice helps to bridge the gap between our waking and dreaming lives.

Dreams also act as a healing balm for the soul, offering comfort and reassurance during turmoil or grief. They can be visits from lost loved ones, reassurances from the universe, or manifestations of our inner strength and resilience.

Shared dreams or similar themes appearing in the dreams of different individuals can indicate a collective consciousness or shared spiritual journey. These shared experiences can be profoundly affirming, suggesting that our journeys are part of a larger, interconnected tapestry.

Finally, dreams and visions invite us to consider the nature of reality itself. They challenge the boundaries of what we think is possible, opening our minds to the idea that there is much more to the universe than what we perceive with our five senses. In this realization, we find the courage to explore the unknown and the wisdom to understand the messages our dreams and visions impart.

In exploring "Emotional Unfolding," we traverse the landscape of our inner feelings, where emotions are not mere responses but gateways to deeper understanding. This journey is an intricate dance with our hearts, where we learn to embrace and decipher the profound messages conveyed by our emotions.

Feelings of joy, sorrow, fear, and love become more than just passing states; they are profound experiences that hold the keys to understanding our deepest selves. Each emotion carries a story, a piece of the puzzle that is our soul. Listening to these stories gives us insights into our deepest desires and fears.

The awakening journey brings with it a heightened sensitivity to emotions. We may find ourselves moved to tears by a piece of music, overwhelmed with joy at a simple act of kindness, or suddenly gripped by fear without an apparent cause. These intensified emotional experiences are not signs of weakness but of our growing connection to the deeper currents of life.

Anger and frustration, often seen as negative emotions, are acknowledged as vital messengers. They alert us to areas in our lives that need attention or change. Recognizing and understanding our anger, we unlock the necessary energy for transformation and growth.

While challenging, feelings of loneliness and isolation catalyze deep introspection. In these moments, we are invited to turn inward, to connect with our innermost selves, and to find solace and strength in our own company. These periods of solitude become fertile grounds for spiritual growth.

Love and compassion take on new depths as we embark on this emotional journey. We begin to experience these feelings not just for others but also for ourselves. Self-love and self-compassion become foundational to our well-being and growth, allowing us to extend the same depth of love to others.

Fear, particularly the fear of the unknown, becomes a companion on our journey. Instead of shying away, we learn to face it with courage and curiosity. In doing so, we often find that our fears are gateways to unexplored parts of ourselves, waiting to be understood and integrated.

Joy becomes a sacred experience, a direct connection to the divine. In moments of pure pleasure, we touch the essence of our being, feeling our interconnectedness with all of existence. These moments are glimpses of enlightenment, showing us the beauty and potential of our true nature.

Grief and sorrow, while painful, are honored as profound teachers. They remind us of the transitory nature of life and the importance of living fully in the present. We learn empathy and compassion through grief, connecting with the universal experience of loss and transformation.

Lastly, the emotional journey leads us to a place of balance and harmony. We learn to navigate our emotions with grace, understanding that each feeling is a part of the intricate tapestry of our human experience. This balance is not suppression or control but understanding and integration, leading us to more profound peace and wisdom.

Exploring "The Call to Solitude," we venture into the sacred space of stillness and introspection. This call is not a retreat from the world but a journey toward the innermost sanctuary of our being. In solitude, we find a profound connection with ourselves, an essential step in our spiritual evolution.

Solitude offers us a respite from daily life's constant noise and demands. In this quiet space, we hear the whispers of our souls, guiding us toward deeper truths. In these moments of stillness, we can connect with the essence of our being, free from the distractions of the external world.

The call to solitude often arrives at pivotal moments in our lives. It might come during periods of transition, loss, or deep questioning. It is an invitation to pause and reflect, to gather our inner resources and gain clarity on our path. This call is a gift, allowing us to realign with our true purpose and essence.

In the embrace of solitude, we engage in deep self-reflection. We explore the landscapes of our mind and heart, uncovering desires, fears, and dreams hidden beneath the surface. This exploration is not always easy, but it is a necessary part of our spiritual journey.

Solitude teaches us the art of being comfortable with our own company. We learn to enjoy our presence, finding peace and contentment within. This self-companionship is a powerful antidote to the feelings of loneliness and dependency that often plague our modern existence.

The practice of meditation flourishes in solitude. Here, we can delve deep into our consciousness, exploring and expanding our understanding of the self and the universe. Meditation becomes a bridge between the soul and the divine, a pathway to transcendence and enlightenment.

Solitude allows us to disconnect from the external influences that shape our thoughts and beliefs. In this space, we can examine and question these influences, developing a more transparent, more authentic understanding of our values and beliefs. This clarity is essential for living a life that is true to ourselves.

In the silence of solitude, we often find the most profound creativity and inspiration. Freed from external pressures and distractions, our minds can wander and explore new ideas and possibilities. This creative freedom is a wellspring for innovation, artistry, and self-expression.

Solitude is not about isolation but building a deeper connection with the world. By understanding ourselves better, we can engage with others more meaningfully and authentically. Our relationships become more prosperous and more fulfilling as a result.

Finally, the call to solitude is a journey that cycles through our lives. We enter solitude, gain insight and wisdom, and then return to the world to share our discoveries and experiences. Each cycle deepens our understanding and connection to ourselves and the universe.

In the mystical journey of "The Dissolution of Ego," we embark on the challenging yet liberating path of shedding the layers of our constructed self. This process is not about losing our identity but uncovering the essence beneath the ego's façade. It's a journey toward authentic self-realization.

The ego, often misunderstood, is not an enemy but a part of our human experience. It is the identity we construct, the roles we play, and the masks we wear. However, in pursuing spiritual growth, we recognize the need to transcend the ego to uncover the unchanging truth of who we are at our core.

This dissolution begins with awareness. We observe how the ego operates and influences our thoughts, emotions, and actions. This self-awareness is the first step in loosening the ego's grip, allowing us to see beyond its illusions.

We encounter the ego's resistance as we delve deeper into this process. The ego clings to familiar patterns and fears the unknown. It resists change, often using fear to keep us within the confines of what is known and comfortable. Recognizing this resistance is crucial as it signifies the points where we are ready to grow.

In this journey, we learn to embrace humility. We realize that much of what we believe to be true about ourselves and the world is limited by the ego's perspective. This humility is not about self-deprecation but about opening ourselves to a broader, more inclusive understanding of existence.

Practicing mindfulness and meditation becomes a powerful tool in dissolving the ego. In stillness, we can observe the ego's narratives without getting caught up. We learn to separate our true selves from the stories and labels that the ego has created.

Love and compassion play a vital role in this process. As we dissolve the barriers of the ego, our capacity for love expands. We start to see others and ourselves in a more compassionate light, recognizing the shared human experience beyond the ego's judgments and separations.

Letting go of attachment is a crucial aspect of dissolving the ego. We release our attachment to outcomes, perceptions, and material possessions. This letting go is not about renunciation but finding freedom from the ego's need for control and approval.

The dissolution of the ego brings a sense of liberation. We experience a newfound freedom in being our authentic selves, unbound by the constraints and expectations of the ego. In this freedom, we find a deeper connection with the essence of our being.

Finally, as the ego dissolves, we experience a profound sense of unity with all that is. The boundaries that once separated us from the rest of existence fade away. We realize that we are not isolated but integral parts of a vast, interconnected whole. This realization is the essence of spiritual awakening, the ultimate liberation from the ego's limitations.

In the profound exploration of "Crisis as a Catalyst," we delve into the transformative power of life's most challenging moments. These crises, often perceived as obstacles, are, in truth, sacred opportunities for growth and awakening. They are the universe urging us to understand our true nature and purpose.

During times of crisis, the very foundations of our beliefs and understandings are shaken. This upheaval, while distressing, serves a higher purpose. It dismantles the illusions and false structures we have built, revealing a more authentic reality beneath. In this revelation, we find the seeds of profound spiritual growth.

We discover that within the heart of every crisis lies a hidden gift. These challenges force us out of our comfort zones, pushing us to tap into inner strengths and resources we might not have known we possessed. Through this process, we uncover aspects of ourselves that were previously hidden in the shadows.

In facing crises, we learn the art of surrender. This surrender is not about giving up; it's about releasing our tight grip on control and opening ourselves to the flow of life. In this space of surrender, we often find clarity and direction, guided by a higher wisdom that transcends our limited understanding.

Crises bring about a stripping away of the non-essential, revealing what truly matters in our lives. We must reevaluate our priorities and values, leading to a life more aligned with our soul's purpose. This realignment is a crucial step in our spiritual evolution.

These times of turmoil are often when we experience the most profound spiritual awakenings. The chaos of the outer world drives us to seek peace within, leading us to explore the depths of our inner world. In this exploration, we encounter the divine essence within each of us.

Crises teach us the power of resilience and the impermanence of all things. We learn to flow with the changes, embracing the cyclical nature of life. This understanding brings peace and the ability to withstand life's ebb and flow gracefully and composure.

The empathy and compassion we develop through our struggles become channels for connecting with others. Our experiences allow us to relate to the pain and challenges of others, fostering a sense of unity and shared humanity. This connection is the heart of genuine compassion and service.

In these moments of crisis, we often find that the most incredible support comes from a place of stillness within. As we quiet the mind and connect with our inner self, we tap into a source of wisdom and strength that guides us through the storm. This inner sanctuary becomes our refuge and our guide.

Lastly, as we emerge from crises, we often find that we have undergone a profound transformation. We are not the same people who entered the storm; we are wiser, stronger, and more authentic. These transformations are the gifts of our struggles, the precious jewels forged in the crucible of our challenges.

In the mystical journey of "Spiritual Stirrings," we delve into the subtle awakenings of our soul, moments where we become acutely aware of a deeper reality pulsating through our existence. These stirrings are gentle nudges from the universe, calling us to explore the vast landscapes of the spirit.

We begin to sense an invisible thread connecting all life, a divine tapestry in which we are intricately woven. This realization is not intellectual but deeply experiential, felt in the core of our being. It is an awakening to the unity of all, a profound understanding that we are part of something much larger and more magnificent than ourselves.

In these moments of spiritual stirring, we find our intuition heightened. We start to trust this inner guidance more, seeing it as an unerring compass that leads us toward truth and authenticity. This intuition speaks in the language of the soul beyond words, guiding us through feelings, insights, and synchronicities.

Nature speaks to us more clearly during these times. The rustling of leaves, the flow of water, the dance of flames - all become symbols carrying messages from the divine. We begin to live in a more harmonious rhythm with the natural world, recognizing it as a living, breathing manifestation of the spiritual realm.

Our dreams become more vivid and insightful, offering us glimpses into the deeper layers of our psyche. They become more than nighttime reveries; they are experiences filled with symbols and messages guiding us on our spiritual path. These dreams are our subconscious mind's way of communicating profound truths.

We start to notice the presence of a higher power in our lives, a benevolent force guiding and supporting us. This might manifest as being watched over, a series of fortunate events, or a sense of inner peace amidst chaos. This presence reassures us that we are never truly alone.

Moments of profound clarity and understanding punctuate our daily lives. Suddenly, truths that once seemed hidden are illuminated, as if the universe has pulled back the veil for us to see. These epiphanies are signposts on our spiritual journey, affirming that we are on the right path.

We develop a more profound sense of empathy and connection with others. This empathy transcends mere emotional response; it is a soul-level connection where we genuinely feel the joys and sorrows of others as our own. This interconnectedness is a fundamental aspect of our spiritual evolution.

Meditation and prayer become more profound and meaningful. In these practices, we connect with the divine, experiencing moments of transcendence where the boundaries between self and the universe blur. These experiences are not escapism but a deeper immersion into the true nature of reality.

Lastly, in these spiritual stirrings, we find a call to action. It is not enough to experience these awakenings; we must live them out in our daily lives. This might manifest as changes in how we live, work, and relate to others. Our spiritual awakenings catalyze us to live more conscious, compassionate, and meaningful lives.

In the profound exploration of "The First Step on the Path," we stand at the precipice of a transformative journey. This initial step is a physical action and a deep, soulful commitment to embark on the quest for spiritual enlightenment and self-discovery. It marks the beginning of a journey that transcends the mundane and ventures into the extraordinary.

We find ourselves at this threshold often after moments of profound realization or deep questioning. A stirring within signals that it is time to seek more, to delve into the mysteries of our existence and the universe. This calling is not heard with the ears but felt with the heart, a resonant vibration that aligns us with our higher purpose.

This first step is an act of courage. It involves stepping into the unknown, leaving behind familiar shores for uncharted waters. The path ahead is not always clear, and the destination is unknown, but the journey promises growth, wisdom, and an expansion of our very being.

As we take this step, we shed layers of our former selves. Beliefs, habits, and patterns that no longer serve us start to fall away. This shedding is vital, allowing new insights, experiences, and truths to take root and flourish.

In this journey, we become seekers of truth. We open ourselves to new perspectives and wisdom from various sources – ancient texts, nature, spiritual teachers, and the whispers of our intuition. Each source offers a piece of the grand puzzle of existence, guiding us deeper into understanding.

We start to see the world with new eyes. The ordinary becomes extraordinary as we notice the magic and beauty in everyday life. A sunrise, a tree, a smile becomes a moment of connection, a reminder of the sacredness of existence.

This step initiates an inward journey to discover our true essence. We seek to understand our inner world, deepest desires, fears, and dreams. This self-discovery is not just self-indulgence but essential to understanding our place in the universe.

The first step on the path often leads to significant changes in our lives. Priorities shift, relationships evolve, and our life's purpose becomes more evident. These changes are not always easy but necessary for our growth and evolution.

We learn to embrace the present moment, understanding that the journey is not about reaching a destination but about each step in awareness and growth. The present moment becomes our teacher, filled with lessons, opportunities, and blessings.

Lastly, this first step is just the beginning of a lifelong journey. It is not a race to the finish but a meandering path with twists and turns, each offering lessons and experiences. We embrace the journey with an open heart and mind, ready to await transformation and enlightenment.

Chapter 2

In "The Seeker's Path," we delve into the essence of embarking on a spiritual quest. This path is not just a physical journey but a deep, inner exploration of the soul. It is a commitment to uncovering the truths that lie beyond the material world, an odyssey into the realms of the mystical and metaphysical.

The seeker begins this journey with a sense of wonder and a thirst for knowledge. The world becomes a canvas of mysteries waiting to be uncovered, each experience and encounter offering a clue to the giant puzzle of existence. An insatiable curiosity drives the seeker to understand the deeper meaning of life.

This path is often sparked by a profound experience or realization, a moment where the mundane veil of everyday life lifts to reveal a glimpse of something more. It could be a moment of awe in nature, a profound sense of connection, or a sudden awareness of a deeper reality. These experiences are the calling cards of the spiritual journey.

The seeker embarks on this path humbly, understanding that the journey is as important as the destination. There is an acknowledgment that wisdom cannot be rushed, that it unfolds in its own time and way. The seeker embraces the journey with patience and an open heart.

As the journey progresses, the seeker finds that the path is not always clear or easy. There are moments of doubt, confusion, and loneliness. Yet, these challenges are essential parts of the journey, offering opportunities for growth and deeper understanding. They are the trials that test and strengthen the seeker's resolve.

In seeking, there is a gradual detachment from material desires and superficial concerns. The seeker begins to find joy and fulfillment in the intangible – in the beauty of a sunset, the wisdom of a well-written book, or the peace of a meditative moment. This shift in perspective is a sign of spiritual maturation.

The seeker often finds guidance in various forms – through teachers, books, nature, and even through synchronistic events. Each of these guides offers insights and lessons that are integral to the seeker's journey. The seeker learns to listen and learn from these guides, understanding that each has a role in their spiritual evolution.

Meditation becomes a vital tool on this path. It is through meditation that the seeker connects with their inner self and the universe. In the silence of meditation, the seeker finds clarity, peace, and insights that are not accessible in the hustle and bustle of everyday life.

The seeker's journey is marked by moments of profound revelation and enlightenment. These moments are often unexpected, revealing transformative truths about the self and the universe. The milestones mark the seeker's progress on their spiritual path.

Finally, the seeker understands that this journey is a lifelong process. There is no final destination, no ultimate enlightenment. Instead, the path is a continuous unfolding of understanding and growth, an eternal journey into the depths of the soul and the mysteries of the universe.

In the profound quest for "Understanding the Cosmic Dance," the seeker embarks on a journey to comprehend the intricate interplay of the universe. This journey is about understanding the physical cosmos and perceiving the subtle energies and rhythms that animate the whole of existence.

The seeker begins to see the universe not as a collection of separate entities but as a harmonious dance of interconnected energies. Stars, planets, life forms, and the vast emptiness of space are all part of a grand, cosmic ballet choreographed by unseen forces. This perception shifts the seeker's understanding from isolation to interconnectedness.

This journey brings with it an awe-inspiring sense of scale and complexity. The vastness of the universe and the intricate beauty of its workings evoke a deep sense of wonder and humility. The seeker realizes that human knowledge is just a drop in the ocean of cosmic wisdom.

The seeker learns to listen to the universe's rhythm, understanding that it resonates within their being. This rhythm is found in the cycles of nature, the movement of the stars, and the flow of life itself. Tuning into this rhythm brings harmony and alignment with the larger order of the universe.

In this quest, ancient pearls of wisdom and modern sciences converge. The seeker finds valuable insights in both the mystical teachings of old and the discoveries of contemporary science. Both are seen as different languages speaking of the same underlying reality.

The seeker discovers the power of intuition to understand the cosmic dance. Beyond logic and reason, intuition taps into a deeper, universal source of knowledge, offering guidance and insight that transcends the limitations of the intellect.

Meditation and contemplative practices become gateways to experiencing the cosmic dance firsthand. In these moments of stillness, the boundaries between the self and the universe begin to dissolve, revealing a direct experience of oneness with all that is.

The seeker finds that the cosmic dance is both external and internal. The universe is mirrored within each individual, and by understanding their inner universe, the seeker gains insight into the larger cosmos. This inner journey is as vast and profound as the journey through the stars.

Synchronicities and meaningful coincidences become signs of the cosmic dance's intricate patterning. These experiences reinforce the understanding that there is a deeper order and intelligence at work, orchestrating the events of our lives in ways that are often beyond our comprehension.

Finally, the seeker understands their role in the cosmic dance is significant and humble. Each action, thought, and intention contributes to the ongoing creation and evolution of the universe. This understanding brings a sense of responsibility and purpose, inspiring the seeker to live in harmony with the cosmic dance, contributing to its beauty and harmony.

In exploring "Embracing the Mystery," the seeker encounters the profound realization that not all of existence can be understood or explained through logic and reason. Accepting the unknown is a pivotal moment on the spiritual path, marking a shift from a solely rational approach to a more holistic, mystical understanding of life. The seeker begins to appreciate that mystery does not equate to confusion or ignorance but represents a deeper layer of truth that transcends conventional knowledge. True wisdom and understanding can be found in these uncharted unknown waters, offering a richer, more nuanced view of the universe and our place.

The journey begins with acknowledging that mystery is an integral part of the universe. The seeker realizes that mystery is not something to be solved but to be experienced and revered. The potential for growth, wonder, and spiritual expansion lies in the spaces of the unknown. This reverence for the unknown encourages a humble acceptance of our limitations and an openness to experiences that defy conventional explanations. It allows the seeker to embrace paradox and ambiguity, understanding that these are not obstacles to spiritual growth but essential aspects of enlightenment.

In embracing mystery, the seeker learns to live with questions that do not have immediate or clear answers. These questions become companions on the journey, guiding the seeker deeper into introspection and discovery. The quest is no longer about finding definitive answers but about learning to thrive in the realm of possibilities. This shift in perspective transforms the seeker's approach to life, instilling a sense of peace and wonder in the face of the unknown. It fosters a mindset that finds joy in exploration and discovery rather than frustration in the lack of closure.

The seeker finds beauty in the inexplicable. The mysteries of life – the birth of a star, the intricacies of love, the depths of the soul – are not seen as puzzles to be solved but as wonders to be marveled at. This shift in perspective brings a sense of awe and reverence for the complexity and majesty of the universe. It cultivates a profound gratitude and respect for the natural world and the intricate web of life that connects us all. The seeker learns to see the world with the eyes of a child, where every moment is a miracle, and every experience is infused with magic.

There is a realization that mystery is not separate from us but is a part of our very nature. The seeker understands that just as there are unknown aspects of the universe, there are also unexplored territories within themselves. The journey of self-discovery is intertwined with accepting one's inner mysteries. This realization opens up new pathways of self-exploration and personal growth, encouraging the seeker to delve into their subconscious, explore their dreams, and confront their hidden fears and desires.

In exploring "Embracing the Mystery," the seeker encounters the profound realization that not all of existence can be understood or explained through logic and reason. Accepting the unknown is a pivotal moment on the spiritual path, marking a shift from a solely rational approach to a more holistic, mystical understanding of life. The seeker begins to appreciate that mystery does not equate to confusion or ignorance but represents a deeper layer of truth that transcends conventional knowledge. True wisdom and understanding can be found in these uncharted unknown waters, offering a richer, more nuanced view of the universe and our place.

The journey begins with acknowledging that mystery is an integral part of the universe. The seeker realizes that mystery is not something to be solved but to be experienced and revered. The potential for growth, wonder, and spiritual expansion lies in the spaces of the unknown. This reverence for the unknown encourages a humble acceptance of our limitations and an openness to experiences that defy conventional explanations. It allows the seeker to embrace paradox and ambiguity, understanding that these are not obstacles to spiritual growth but essential aspects of enlightenment.

In embracing mystery, the seeker learns to live with questions that do not have immediate or clear answers. These questions become companions on the journey, guiding the seeker deeper into introspection and discovery. The quest is no longer about finding definitive answers but about learning to thrive in the realm of possibilities. This shift in perspective transforms the seeker's approach to life, instilling a sense of peace and wonder in the face of the unknown. It fosters a mindset that finds joy in exploration and discovery rather than frustration in the lack of closure.

The seeker finds beauty in the inexplicable. The mysteries of life – the birth of a star, the intricacies of love, the depths of the soul – are not seen as puzzles to be solved but as wonders to be marveled at. This shift in perspective brings a sense of awe and reverence for the complexity and majesty of the universe. It cultivates a profound gratitude and respect for the natural world and the intricate web of life that connects us all. The seeker learns to see the world with the eyes of a child, where every moment is a miracle, and every experience is infused with magic.

There is a realization that mystery is not separate from us but is a part of our very nature. The seeker understands that just as there are unknown aspects of the universe, there are also unexplored territories within themselves. The journey of self-discovery is intertwined with accepting one's inner mysteries. This realization opens up new pathways of self-exploration and personal growth, encouraging the seeker to delve into their subconscious, explore their dreams, and confront their hidden fears and desires.

The mystical experience becomes a valuable source of knowledge and insight. Beyond the reach of empirical evidence and logical deduction, mystical experiences offer a direct, personal encounter with the divine. These experiences are profoundly transformative, providing glimpses into the true nature of reality. They defy conventional understanding and profoundly speak to the heart and soul. These moments of transcendence are often ineffable, yet they leave an indelible mark on the seeker's consciousness, reshaping their perception of reality and their understanding of themselves.

In embracing mystery, the seeker develops a profound trust in life's journey. There is an understanding that some things are beyond human control and comprehension and that surrendering to the flow of life is an act of faith and wisdom. This trust is not passive resignation but an active engagement with life in all its complexity. It involves embracing uncertainty and finding joy and meaning in the journey, regardless of twists and turns.

The seeker engages with ancient wisdom and spiritual traditions, finding that they often speak the language of mystery. These traditions offer symbolic and allegorical teachings that open the door to deeper understanding, guiding the seeker through the realms of the unknown. Exploring ancient wisdom provides a sense of continuity and connection with the past, offering timeless insights and practices that have guided countless seekers. It also fosters a sense of belonging to a larger community of seekers across cultures and generations.

Meditation and contemplative practices deepen the seeker's relationship with mystery. In the silence of deep meditation, the seeker encounters the ineffable, the indescribable aspects of existence. These moments of communion with the mysterious are profound and life-changing. They provide a direct experience of the interconnectedness of all things and a sense of oneness with the universe. This deep connection nourishes the soul and offers inner peace and contentment.

Lastly, the seeker finds that embracing mystery is an act of liberation. It frees them from the need to know and control everything, allowing them to live with greater ease, joy, and wonder. The acceptance of mystery becomes a source of strength and peace, grounding the seeker in the present moment and opening their heart to the infinite wonders of existence. This liberation is not just a personal achievement; it radiates outward, influencing the seeker's interactions with others and their approach to life's challenges. In embracing the unknown, the seeker becomes a beacon of hope and inspiration, showing others the beauty and richness that lies in the heart of the mystery.

In the pursuit of "Seeking Universal Wisdom," the seeker delves into the rich tapestry of knowledge that transcends time and culture. This quest is not merely for information but for the profound wisdom that connects and underpins the myriad expressions of life and existence. The seeker becomes a bridge between the ancient and the modern, the seen and the unseen, seeking truths that resonate with the core of their being.

The journey involves exploring the teachings of sages, mystics, and philosophers from diverse cultures and epochs. Each tradition offers unique insights into the nature of reality, the human experience, and the divine. The seeker finds that, despite the apparent differences in language and metaphor, there is a common thread of understanding that weaves through all these teachings.

In seeking universal wisdom, the seeker develops a profound respect for the interconnectedness of all knowledge. They understand that science and spirituality, reason and intuition, the practical and the mystical are not opposing forces but complementary aspects of a single, grand tapestry of understanding. This holistic view fosters a more integrated approach to knowledge and existence.

The light of inquiry and openness illuminates the seeker's path. They approach each new piece of wisdom with curiosity and a willingness to learn, unburdened by preconceived notions or dogmatic beliefs. This openness allows them to absorb knowledge in its purest form, untainted by bias or ego.

The exploration of universal wisdom often leads the seeker into the realms of paradox and mystery. They discover that true wisdom often lies in embracing the unknowable, understanding that the essence of some truths cannot be captured in words or concepts. This realization deepens their appreciation for the mystical aspects of existence.

Meditation and contemplative practices become essential tools in this quest. They provide a space for the seeker to digest and integrate the wisdom they encounter, allowing insights to emerge deep within their consciousness. These practices help in grounding abstract and lofty concepts into personal, experiential knowledge.

The seeker finds that the pursuit of wisdom is also an inward journey. As they explore external teachings and philosophies, they are simultaneously guided to confront their inner truths, biases, and misconceptions. This inner exploration is as challenging as it is rewarding, leading to personal growth and transformation.

Throughout this journey, the seeker learns to balance the pursuit of knowledge with the practice of wisdom. They understand that true wisdom is about acquiring information, living, and embodying the truths they discover. It involves applying these teachings in everyday life, allowing them to shape one's actions, decisions, and interactions.

The seeker's quest for universal wisdom is a journey without end. Each answer leads to new questions, and each insight opens the door to further exploration. The seeker embraces this never-ending journey, finding joy in expanding understanding and consciousness.

Finally, the seeker understands that their pursuit of universal wisdom is not just for personal enlightenment but for the benefit of all. They become a vessel through which this wisdom flows into the world, sharing insights, inspiring others, and contributing to humanity's collective growth and evolution. In seeking knowledge, they become a beacon of light, guiding others on their paths of discovery and understanding.

In exploring "The Wisdom of Stillness," the seeker discovers the profound depth and insights in moments of serenity and inaction. This stillness is not an absence but a rich, fertile ground for spiritual and personal growth. In the quiet, the seeker finds a connection to the inner self and the universe that is often lost in the noise of everyday life.

The journey into stillness begins with the understanding that true wisdom often speaks in whispers, in the soft, subtle language of the soul. The seeker learns to quiet the mind, to listen beyond the chatter of thoughts and the distractions of the external world. They find clarity and insight in this quietness as if the universe is whispering its secrets.

The practice of meditation becomes a key to unlocking the wisdom of stillness. Through meditation, the seeker learns to cultivate a state of inner tranquility, where the mind is calm and the heart is open. This state allows them to access more profound levels of consciousness and understanding, connecting them with a wellspring of inner wisdom.

In the stillness, the seeker begins to perceive the subtle energies that animate all of existence. They become attuned to the rhythm of life, the ebb and flow of the cosmos. This attunement brings a profound sense of harmony and alignment with the universe, a feeling of being in the right place at the right time.

The wisdom of stillness teaches the seeker about the power of presence. They learn that being fully present in the moment, fully engaged with the now, is a source of immense strength and clarity. This presence is not just a state of mind but a way of being, a practice that transforms every aspect of their life.

In embracing stillness, the seeker discovers the value of patience. They understand that not all questions need immediate answers and that some truths unfold in their own time. This patience is not passive waiting but an active engagement with the process of life, a trust in the natural unfolding of events.

The stillness becomes a sanctuary, a place of refuge and rejuvenation. In times of turmoil or confusion, the seeker retreats into this inner haven, finding peace and stability amidst the chaos. This sanctuary is always available, a constant source of comfort and support.

Through stillness, the seeker explores the depths of their being. They confront their fears, their hopes, and their dreams. This self-exploration is a journey to the heart of their identity, a quest to understand who they are beyond the labels and roles imposed by society.

The wisdom of stillness also brings a deeper appreciation for the simple things in life. The seeker finds joy and beauty in the ordinary, in the subtle play of light, the gentle rustle of leaves, and the warmth of a smile. This appreciation is a form of mindfulness, a recognition of the sacredness of everyday existence.

Lastly, the seeker realizes that the wisdom of stillness is a gift to be shared. They become a beacon of calm and clarity in a world often filled with noise and haste. By embodying the principles of stillness, they inspire others to seek their inner peace, spreading the profound insights found in the quiet to the world around them.

In delving into "The Art of Inner Listening," the seeker embarks on a journey to tune into their inner self's subtle, often overlooked voice. This art is a profound practice of attuning to the whispers of the soul, deciphering the messages conveyed not through words but through feelings, intuition, and the quiet stirrings of the heart.

The journey begins with recognizing the noise dominating our internal and external environments. The seeker learns to differentiate between the cacophony of everyday thoughts, societal expectations, and more profound, more authentic inner guidance. This discernment is the first step towards truly understanding and valuing the insights from within.

Inner listening involves cultivating a mindful presence, fully attentive to the current moment and the nuances of one's internal experience. In this state, the seeker becomes receptive to the subtle intuitions and gut feelings that often guide us more accurately than our logical minds. This mindfulness is not a passive state but an active engagement with the self.

Meditation becomes a crucial tool in honing the art of inner listening. Through meditation, the seeker learns to quiet the mind and create a space of stillness where the inner voice can be heard more clearly. This practice is not about silencing thoughts but finding the space between thoughts where true wisdom resides.

In inner listening, the seeker encounters the body's deep wisdom. They learn to listen to the body's physical sensations and signals, understanding that these are often direct messages from the subconscious mind. This bodily wisdom is a compass guiding the seeker toward health, alignment, and balance.

The seeker discovers that inner listening is an ongoing dialogue with the self. It involves asking questions, seeking guidance, and patiently waiting for the responses from within. This dialogue fosters a deeper relationship with oneself, built on trust and understanding.

Inner listening also opens the door to receiving guidance from the universe. The seeker finds that the more they listen to their inner self, the more they become attuned to the synchronicities and signs of the universe. These external confirmations serve as affirmations of the inner wisdom being received.

The art of inner listening teaches the seeker the value of silence and solitude. In quiet and alone time, the distractions of the external world fade away, allowing a more profound connection with the inner self. These moments of solitude become sacred spaces for self-discovery and reflection.

Through inner listening, the seeker learns to navigate life's challenges with greater ease and insight. They find that the answers they seek are often already within them, waiting to be uncovered. This realization brings a sense of empowerment and independence, as the seeker understands they are their best guide.

Finally, the seeker realizes that inner listening is a lifelong practice. It evolves and deepens over time, offering endless insight and understanding. By committing to this practice, the seeker enhances their life and brings a more profound sense of presence and wisdom to their interactions with others, becoming a conduit of inner peace and clarity in a chaotic world.

In exploring "Embracing Life's Paradoxes," the seeker encounters the intricate dance of contradictions that life often presents. This journey is about understanding that paradoxes are not hurdles to be overcome but mysteries to be embraced. They are the universe's way of teaching us the complexity and depth of existence, revealing that truth often resides in the harmony of opposites.

The seeker begins to appreciate that life is a blend of light and shadow, strength and vulnerability, movement and stillness. Instead of seeking to resolve these paradoxes, they learn to hold them in balance. This equilibrium is not about choosing one aspect over the other but understanding that both are essential parts of the whole.

In embracing paradoxes, the seeker discovers the fluid nature of reality. They understand that what appears contradictory on the surface often has an underlying unity. This realization opens the mind to a broader perspective, where the duality of right and wrong, good and bad, becomes less rigid, allowing for a more nuanced and inclusive understanding of life.

The art of inner listening is crucial in navigating life's paradoxes. The seeker learns to tune into the wisdom of their heart and soul, which often understands the complexities of life better than the rational mind. This inner guidance helps reconcile the seemingly conflicting aspects of experiences and insights.

Meditation and contemplative practices deepen the seeker's relationship with paradoxes. In the stillness of meditation, the boundaries between opposing forces begin to blur, revealing a more profound unity. The seeker finds that the noise of contradictions settles into a harmonious symphony of existence in the silence.

The seeker learns to embrace uncertainty and ambiguity, recognizing them as fertile grounds for growth and insight. They find that the most profound lessons often come from sitting with the unknown without rushing to discover answers or resolutions. This comfort with uncertainty fosters a deep sense of trust in life's journey.

Life's paradoxes teach the seeker about the beauty of imperfection. They learn to embrace their flaws and contradictions, understanding that perfection is not a state to be achieved but a myth to be dispelled. In this acceptance, they find a greater sense of authenticity and freedom.

The seeker finds that paradoxes are intellectual concepts and lived experiences. They witness these paradoxes in their relationships, aspirations, and inner struggles. Each encounter with a paradox becomes an opportunity for deeper self-awareness and wisdom.

Through embracing paradoxes, the seeker develops a profound empathy and compassion for others. They understand that everyone is navigating their own set of contradictions and challenges. This empathy breaks down barriers of judgment and separation, fostering a sense of shared humanity.

Lastly, the seeker realizes that embracing life's paradoxes is an ongoing journey. It is a path that requires continual openness, reflection, and balance. By acknowledging and living with paradoxes, the seeker embodies a wisdom that is fluid and adaptable, capable of holding the many truths of life in a compassionate embrace.

In exploring "The Dance of Change and Transformation," the seeker embarks on a journey to embrace the constant flux of life. This exploration delves into understanding that change is not a force to be resisted but an essential aspect of existence to be adopted. The seeker learns that transformation is the universe's way of unfolding new possibilities and paths, guiding us toward growth and self-realization.

The seeker begins to appreciate that change is the only constant in life. Instead of clinging to the familiar and the known, they learn to flow with the currents of transformation. This fluidity allows them to navigate life's changes with grace and resilience, understanding that each shift brings opportunities for new experiences and insights.

Embracing change involves letting go of the fear of the unknown. The seeker realizes that fear often stems from a desire for control and predictability. By releasing this need for control, they open themselves to the full spectrum of life's experiences, finding beauty and wisdom even in uncertainty and impermanence.

The art of inner listening becomes a valuable tool in understanding and navigating change. The seeker learns to trust their intuition and inner guidance, which often provide clarity and direction amidst the chaos of transformation. This inner listening fosters a deep sense of trust in oneself and life's journey.

Meditation and contemplative practices offer a sanctuary of stability within the whirlwind of change. In these moments of stillness, the seeker finds a center of calm and balance. This inner equilibrium provides the strength and perspective to embrace external changes with an open heart and mind.

The seeker discovers the transformative power of embracing their cycles of change. They recognize the patterns of growth, stagnation, and renewal in their own life. This awareness allows them to work harmoniously with these cycles, honoring each phase for the unique gifts and challenges it brings.

Change and transformation are seen as processes of shedding and renewal. The seeker learns to let go of old beliefs, habits, and identities that no longer serve them, making space for new aspects of themselves to emerge. This shedding is not a loss but a liberation, freeing them to evolve into a fuller expression of their true self.

The dance of change teaches the seeker about the interconnectedness of all things. They see how changes in one area of life ripple out to affect others and how their transformation impacts the world around them. This understanding fosters a sense of responsibility and mindfulness in their actions and choices.

Through the journey of change and transformation, the seeker develops a sense of resilience and adaptability. They learn to find stability within themselves rather than in external circumstances. This inner strength allows them to face life's changes with courage and optimism.

Lastly, the seeker recognizes that the dance of change and transformation is an endless, eternal process. They come to celebrate each twist and turn of the journey, finding joy in the continuous unfolding of their life story. By embracing change, the seeker becomes a co-creator with the universe, actively participating in the magnificent dance of existence.

In delving into "The Quest for Inner Harmony," the seeker embarks on a profound journey to find balance and peace within themselves. This quest is about achieving momentary calm and cultivating a deep, lasting inner harmony that resonates through every aspect of their being. The seeker understands this harmony is the key to a fulfilled and meaningful life.

The journey begins with the realization that inner harmony is not found in external circumstances but within the depths of one's soul. The seeker turns their focus inward, exploring their mind, emotions, and spirit landscapes. In this exploration, they seek to understand the intricate interplay of their inner workings and how they can align these.

Embracing inner harmony involves acknowledging and accepting all parts of oneself. The seeker learns to embrace their light and shadow, understanding that true harmony consists in integrating all aspects of their being. This acceptance does not mean resignation but a deep understanding and love for oneself and one's flaws.

The art of inner listening becomes a critical practice in achieving inner harmony. The seeker tunes into their inner voice and intuition, learning to trust the wisdom from within. This internal guidance system becomes a compass, helping them navigate life's challenges and decisions.

Meditation and mindfulness are essential tools in this quest. Through these practices, the seeker cultivates a state of presence and awareness, allowing them to experience life fully and respond to situations with clarity and balance. These practices also help quiet the mind, creating a space where inner harmony can flourish.

The seeker discovers the power of self-reflection and introspection in maintaining inner harmony. Regular periods of self-examination allow them to stay aligned with their core values and goals. This ongoing process of self-awareness ensures they remain true to themselves and their path.

Embracing inner harmony also involves learning to manage and balance emotions. The seeker develops emotional intelligence, understanding how to navigate their dynamic landscape without being overwhelmed. They remember to express their feelings healthily and constructively, contributing to their well-being.

The quest for inner harmony is also a journey of letting go of control and surrendering to the flow of life. The seeker learns that controlling every aspect of life is futile and stressful. Instead, they embrace flexibility and openness, trusting in the journey and gracefully accepting twists and turns.

In seeking inner harmony, the seeker finds that relationships and interactions with others also become more harmonious. They bring a sense of calm, understanding, and balance to their interactions, positively impacting their relationships. This external harmony reflects the peace and balance they have cultivated within.

Finally, the seeker understands that the quest for inner harmony is ongoing. It is not a destination to be reached but a continuous journey of growth and learning. Each day brings new opportunities to deepen this inner harmony, making it a lifelong practice and commitment. Through this quest, the seeker becomes a beacon of peace and stability for themselves and those around them.

Chapter 3

In "Discovering the Silence Within," the seeker embarks on a profound journey into the heart of stillness. This exploration is not merely about experiencing the absence of sound but about connecting with a deep, inner silence beyond the surface noise of daily life. The seeker learns that this silence is the key to profound wisdom and a deeper understanding of the self and the universe.

The journey begins with recognizing that true silence is more than a lack of external noise; it is a profound inner peace and stillness. The seeker starts to cultivate moments of silence in their daily life, creating spaces where they can connect with this tranquil inner realm. This practice involves more than just seeking quiet places; it is about quieting the mind and opening the heart.

As the seeker delves deeper into the silence, they discover a space brimming with potential and insight. In this stillness, the mind's chatter slows down, allowing more profound, intuitive knowledge to emerge. This inner wisdom speaks in a language beyond words, offering guidance and clarity often lost in everyday life's hustle and bustle.

The practice of meditation becomes a vital gateway to accessing this inner silence. Through meditation, the seeker learns to transcend the constant stream of thoughts, worries, and distractions, entering a state of deep peace and connection with the self. This connection provides a sense of grounding and centeredness that carries through all aspects of life.

In the silence, the seeker begins to understand the interconnectedness of all things. They realize that silence is not empty but full of the subtle energy that connects all of existence. This understanding fosters a sense of unity with the world and a more profound empathy for all living beings.

The seeker finds that silence is a source of creativity and inspiration. In the quiet of the mind, new ideas and solutions emerge effortlessly.

This creativity is not forced but flows naturally from the deep well of stillness within, reflecting the seeker's true essence and potential.

Embracing inner silence also leads to a transformation in how the seeker perceives and interacts with the world. They become more present and mindful in their actions and communications, bringing a quality of calm and clarity to their relationships and endeavors.

The journey into silence teaches the seeker about the power of listening. Learning to attend to their inner silence makes them more attuned to the world around them. This attunement allows them to hear not just with their ears but with their heart, understanding the unspoken messages and emotions that underlie words and actions.

As the seeker deepens their relationship with inner silence, they find that it becomes a sanctuary, a place of refuge from the chaos and noise of the world. This sanctuary is always accessible, a source of peace and stability they can turn to in times of stress or uncertainty.

Finally, the seeker realizes that the journey into silence is an ongoing, lifelong practice of deepening their connection with the stillness within. Each encounter with this inner silence brings new insights, growth, and a greater spiritual connection. In discovering the silence within, the seeker taps into a wellspring of wisdom and peace that enriches every aspect of their life, illuminating their path with clarity and serenity.

In exploring "The Power of Nature's Silence," the seeker discovers the profound tranquility and wisdom in the natural world. This journey is not just about enjoying the quiet of a forest or the calm of a mountain but about connecting with the deep, resonant silence that nature embodies. The seeker learns that this silence is a teacher, offering lessons of harmony, resilience, and the interconnectedness of all life.

The journey begins with an appreciation for the subtle sounds of nature - the rustling leaves, the flowing water, the whispering wind. The seeker realizes these sounds are expressions of nature's silence, a symphony of balance and peace. In listening to these natural melodies, the seeker finds their inner noise diminishing, giving way to a profound sense of calm.

As the seeker immerses themselves in natural settings, they feel a deep connection with the earth. This connection goes beyond the physical senses; it is a spiritual communion with the essence of life. The stillness of nature reflects the stillness within, guiding the seeker to a place of inner serenity and understanding.

In the quiet of nature, the seeker learns the art of mindful presence. Surrounded by the timeless beauty of the natural world, they become fully aware of the present moment. This awareness is a gift, revealing the richness of existence and the simple joy of being.

Nature's silence teaches the seeker about the cycles and rhythms of life. Observing the changing seasons, the ebb and flow of tides, and the growth and decay of living things, the seeker understands existence's transient yet eternal nature. This understanding brings a sense of peace and acceptance of life's impermanence.

The seeker finds in nature a reflection of their inner landscapes. The vastness of the sky, the depth of the ocean, and the mountains' strength all mirror the vast, deep, and vital aspects of the human soul. This reflection inspires a journey of self-exploration and discovery rooted in the wisdom of the natural world.

In the silence of nature, the seeker becomes attuned to the subtler aspects of existence. They notice the intricate patterns in leaves, the play of light and shadow, and the dance of insects. This attention to detail is a form of reverence, a recognition of the sacredness of all forms of life.

The natural world also becomes a space for healing and rejuvenation. In the quiet embrace of nature, the seeker finds their stresses and worries melting away, replaced by a sense of wholeness and well-being. This physical and spiritual healing is a holistic nourishment that rejuvenates the soul.

Nature's silence offers profound lessons in resilience and adaptation. Observing how plants and animals thrive in various environments, the seeker learns about the strength and adaptability inherent in all living beings. These lessons inspire the seeker to embrace their challenges with renewed strength and flexibility.

Finally, the seeker understands nature's silence is a profound teacher of interconnectedness. In the web of life, everything is connected, each element supporting and being supported by others. This realization fosters a sense of responsibility and care for the environment as the seeker acknowledges their role in the intricate tapestry of life. By connecting with nature's silence, the seeker deepens their understanding of themselves and their place in the universe, finding peace and purpose in the harmonious silence of the natural world.

In exploring "The Essence of Solitary Reflection," the seeker embarks on a journey of deep self-contemplation. This path is about discovering the profound insights and truths that emerge from introspective solitude. The seeker understands that in the quiet and solitude, the voice of their deepest self becomes clearer, offering wisdom and guidance often obscured by everyday life's noise.

The journey begins with the recognition of solitude as a sacred space. The seeker learns to cherish moments alone as opportunities for profound personal growth and reflection. In these moments of solitude, they confront their innermost thoughts, fears, and aspirations, unfiltered by the distractions and influences of the outside world.

Solitary reflection involves a courageous dive into the depths of one's psyche. The seeker ventures into this inner terrain, not with trepidation but with curiosity and openness. In exploring the landscapes of their mind and heart, they discover hidden aspects of their personality, unacknowledged strengths, and unresolved conflicts.

In these quiet moments, the seeker dialogues with their inner self. This dialogue is not about self-criticism or rumination but seeking understanding and clarity. Questions posed in solitude receive answers from the depths of the seeker's wisdom, answers that resonate with authenticity and truth.

Meditation and mindfulness practices enhance the experience of solitary reflection. These practices help quiet the mind and focus attention, making the inner journey more intentional and insightful. They allow the seeker to observe their thoughts and emotions without judgment, fostering a deeper understanding of their inner workings.

Solitary reflection often leads to moments of epiphany and realization. Insights that elude the seeker in the bustle of daily life suddenly become apparent in the stillness of solitude. These realizations can be transformative, shifting the seeker's perspective and opening new pathways for growth and change.

In embracing solitude, the seeker learns to be comfortable with their company. This comfort is not about isolation but finding a sense of completeness within oneself. It fosters a profound sense of self-reliance and confidence, empowering the seeker in all areas of life.

The solitude also becomes a fertile ground for creativity and inspiration. The seeker's mind can wander and explore new ideas and possibilities free from external distractions and influences. This creative freedom often leads to novel solutions, artistic expressions, and innovative thinking.

The seeker discovers that solitary reflection is not a static state but a dynamic process of growth and evolution. Each session of solitary contemplation builds upon the last, deepening the seeker's understanding of themselves and their place in the world. It is a continual process of unfolding and discovery.

Lastly, the seeker realizes that the insights gained in solitary reflection are not just for personal edification but have the power to transform their interactions with the world. By understanding themselves better, they approach relationships and challenges with greater empathy, clarity, and wisdom. The solitary journey thus enriches the seeker's inner life and engagement with the world, making solitary reflection an integral part of their spiritual and personal development.

In the journey of "Unveiling the Inner Voice," the seeker delves into the art of tuning into their most authentic self. This exploration is not just about recognizing thoughts or emotions but about connecting with the deeper voice that guides and informs one's most genuine expressions and choices. The seeker understands this inner voice is a compass, offering direction and wisdom from their well-being.

The journey begins with distinguishing the inner voice from the noise of everyday thoughts and external influences. The seeker learns to discern between fleeting impulses and their true self's more profound, consistent voice. This voice often speaks gently and guidingly, contrasting with the clamor of conditioned responses and societal expectations.

The seeker cultivates a sense of inner silence and stillness in connecting with their inner voice. They find that in moments of serenity, the inner voice becomes more apparent and accessible. This practice involves more than physical quiet; it is about creating a tranquil space in the mind where the inner voice can be heard clearly.

The seeker discovers that the inner voice is a source of intuitive knowledge and insight. This voice often communicates through feelings, sensations, and sometimes through symbols and dreams. The seeker learns to trust and interpret these messages, recognizing them as guidance from their deepest self.

Meditation and mindfulness practices become essential tools in unveiling the inner voice. Through these practices, the seeker develops the ability to observe their thoughts and emotions without attachment, allowing the inner voice to emerge without interference. This clarity brings the seeker closer to their core truths and intuition.

The inner voice also becomes a guide in personal growth and self-discovery. It gently nudges the seeker towards experiences and decisions that align with their true path and purpose. The seeker learns to listen and follow this guidance, understanding that it leads to authenticity and fulfillment.

In moments of decision and uncertainty, the inner voice becomes a beacon of clarity. The seeker learns to consult this inner wisdom in making choices, big and small. By aligning their decisions with the guidance of the inner voice, the seeker navigates life with greater confidence and harmony.

The seeker finds that the inner voice is not static but evolves with them. As they grow and change, so does the voice, reflecting their ongoing journey of self-realization. This dynamic nature of the inner voice makes it a reliable and relevant guide throughout the seeker's life.

Embracing the inner voice fosters a deep sense of self-trust and self-acceptance. The seeker understands that this voice manifests their true self, and they praise their authenticity by honoring it. This acceptance brings a profound sense of peace and self-assuredness.

Finally, the seeker realizes that the inner voice is a personal guide and connects them to universal wisdom. By tuning into their inner voice, the seeker taps into the collective consciousness, accessing insights and knowledge beyond their individual experience. This connection enriches the seeker's understanding of themselves and their place in the world, making unveiling the inner voice a crucial step in their spiritual and personal journey.

In exploring "Contemplating the Vastness," the seeker embarks on a journey to comprehend the infinite nature of the universe and their place within it. This contemplation is not merely an intellectual exercise but a deep, soulful immersion into the boundless dimensions of existence. The seeker realizes that understanding the vastness is critical to expanding their consciousness and connecting with a greater reality.

The journey begins with an acknowledgment of the sheer scale of the universe. The seeker becomes aware of the vast expanse of space, the countless stars, galaxies, and the unfathomable depths of the cosmos.

This realization brings both a sense of awe and a feeling of humility as they recognize their smallness in the grand scheme of existence.

In contemplating the vastness, the seeker discovers the beauty of insignificance. They understand that while they may be a small part of the vast universe, their existence is still essential and meaningful. This paradoxical understanding brings a sense of peace and belonging as they see themselves as integral threads in the tapestry of the cosmos.

The seeker learns to embrace the unknown and the unknowable. They understand that the vastness of the universe is not just physical but also extends to realms beyond human comprehension. Accepting the unknown is not a resignation but an acknowledgment of existence's limitless potential and mysteries.

Meditation and contemplative practices become gateways to experiencing the vastness. In meditation, the seeker transcends the confines of the physical body and the ego, touching the edges of the infinite. This experience is both humbling and exhilarating as they glimpse the immensity of their true nature.

The vastness teaches the seeker about the interconnectedness of all things. They realize that the universe is a complex, interwoven web of energy and matter, and they are part of this web. This understanding fosters a sense of unity and compassion for all forms of life.

In contemplating the vastness, the seeker grapples with the concept of time – its enormity and illusion. They reflect on the ancientness of the universe and the fleeting nature of human life, understanding that time is a relative, fluid construct that shapes our perception of existence.

The seeker finds that contemplating the vastness brings a new perspective on their problems and challenges. The issues that once seemed overwhelming appear smaller against the backdrop of the infinite cosmos. This perspective brings clarity and a sense of calm in dealing with life's trials.

The vastness also inspires a sense of wonder and curiosity in the seeker. They are driven to learn more, explore further, and understand deeper. This insatiable curiosity fuels their journey, leading them to discoveries and insights about the universe and themselves.

Finally, the seeker realizes that contemplating the vastness is an ongoing journey. Each moment of realization, each glimpse of the infinite, adds to their understanding and connection with the universe. This journey is about seeking answers and embracing the mystery and majesty of existence, allowing the vastness to unfold its wisdom in the seeker's heart and mind.

In the pursuit of "Harmonizing with Cosmic Rhythms," the seeker embarks on a profound journey to align with the natural cycles and patterns that govern the universe. This exploration is not just about understanding these rhythms intellectually but about integrating them into one's life, thus achieving a more profound harmony with the cosmos. The seeker realizes that by attuning to these universal rhythms, they can live in a more balanced, synchronized manner with the world around them.

The journey begins with recognizing the myriad rhythms that orchestrate the universe - the moon's cycles, the ebb and flow of tides, the changing seasons, and even the rhythmic patterns of stars and galaxies. The seeker learns to observe and appreciate these cosmic patterns, understanding their significance in the grand design of existence.

Harmonizing with these rhythms, the seeker discovers the beauty of living in sync with nature. They adapt their lifestyle to mirror natural cycles, finding that this alignment brings a sense of ease and flow into their life. Simple acts like waking with the sun or recognizing the energetic shifts of different seasons become practices of cosmic harmony.

The seeker delves into ancient wisdom and practices that honor cosmic rhythms. They explore traditions like astrology, Ayurveda, and other indigenous knowledge systems emphasizing the importance of living in harmony with the natural world. These practices offer insights into how to align one's life with the rhythms of the cosmos.

Meditation and contemplation become tools for connecting with cosmic rhythms. Through these practices, the seeker attunes their inner being to the subtle energies and cycles of the universe. This inner attunement leads to a deeper understanding of how these rhythms influence their body, mind, and spirit.

The seeker learns to navigate life's ebbs and flows with greater ease. Just as the universe experiences cycles of expansion and contraction, so does the human experience. By recognizing and embracing these personal cycles, the seeker can navigate life's ups and downs with more grace and resilience.

In aligning with cosmic rhythms, the seeker finds a profound sense of timing. They understand that there is a right time for action and a suitable time for rest, a time to grow, and a time to let go. This sense of timing, guided by the rhythms of the universe, brings a sense of harmony and purpose to their actions.

The seeker discovers that cosmic rhythms are not just external phenomena but resonate within them. They begin to see themselves as microcosms of the universe, embodying the same patterns and cycles within their being. This realization fosters a deeper connection with the self and the world.

Harmonizing with cosmic rhythms also involves recognizing the interconnectedness of all life. The seeker understands that their actions have ripple effects throughout the cosmic web. This awareness brings a sense of responsibility and mindfulness to how they live and interact with the world.

Lastly, the seeker realizes that harmonizing with cosmic rhythms is a lifelong journey. It is a continuous process of learning, adapting, and growing in sync with the universe. This journey brings a deep sense of fulfillment and peace as the seeker learns to dance harmoniously with existence's vast, rhythmic symphony.

In the quest for "Embracing the Wisdom of the Elements," the seeker engages with the fundamental forces of nature - earth, air, fire, water, and ether. This journey is about understanding and integrating the qualities of these elemental forces into their being. The seeker realizes that each element offers unique insights and energies that can enhance their spiritual and personal growth.

The journey begins with the earth element, symbolizing stability, strength, and nourishment. The seeker learns to ground themselves in the earth's energy, finding balance and a sense of security. This grounding provides a strong foundation for their spiritual practices and daily life, reminding them of the importance of staying connected to the physical world.

Air represents intellect, communication, and movement. The seeker explores air qualities, learning to embrace change and flexibility in their thoughts and actions. They find their mind become more agile and open by attuning to the air element, fostering creativity and new perspectives.

Fire symbolizes transformation, energy, and passion. The seeker discovers the power of fire to ignite their inner drive and to burn away impurities and obstacles. This elemental force teaches them about the cycles of destruction and rebirth, showing them that new life can emerge from the ashes of the old.

Water represents emotion, intuition, and flow. The seeker delves into the depths of the water element, embracing their emotional nature and the fluidity of life. They learn to move gracefully with life's currents, finding wisdom in their feelings and developing a more profound sense of empathy and connection with others.

The ether or space element represents the vastness, freedom, and spiritual dimension. The seeker learns to expand their awareness, exploring the boundless nature of their consciousness. This element teaches them about the interconnectedness of all things and the infinite possibilities within the silent, expansive space.

In integrating these elements, the seeker finds a sense of wholeness and harmony. They understand that each component is vital and that balancing these forces is essential for well-being. This balance is not static but a dynamic, ongoing process of adaptation and attunement.

The seeker also explores the elemental energies in the natural world, observing how these forces interact and manifest in the environment. They find that by connecting with the elements in nature, they can enhance their understanding and experience of these energies within themselves.

Each element offers a path to self-discovery and transformation. The seeker uses practices such as meditation, visualization, and ritual to connect with and embody the qualities of the elements. These practices help them align with the elemental forces, drawing on their energies for personal growth and spiritual advancement.

The elements also offer a framework for understanding existence's physical and spiritual aspects. The seeker finds that the components are material entities and symbols of deeper spiritual truths. This understanding deepens their connection to the universe and their sense of awe and wonder at the complexity of existence.

Finally, the seeker realizes that the wisdom of the elements is a lifelong journey. Each stage of life and each experience offers new opportunities to engage with and learn from these fundamental forces. By embracing the wisdom of the elements, the seeker weaves a rich tapestry of understanding and connection, uniting the physical and spiritual realms in a dance of harmony and insight.

In the pursuit of "Exploring the Realm of Dreams," the seeker embarks on a mystical journey into the depths of their subconscious. This exploration is about understanding the meanings behind dreams and tapping into the rich, symbolic language through which the soul communicates. The seeker realizes that dreams are not mere figments of the imagination but are windows to deeper truths and hidden aspects of the self.

The journey begins with acknowledging that dreams are a unique form of guidance. The seeker learns to recall and reflect upon their dreams, recognizing them as messages from the deeper layers of their psyche. These messages often come in symbols and scenarios that, upon waking reflection, provide clarity and insight into the seeker's life.

In delving into the dream world, the seeker discovers the fluid nature of reality as perceived by the subconscious. They find that in dreams, the boundaries of time and space are malleable, and the laws of physics are no longer applicable. This realization opens the seeker to new possibilities and understandings of the nature of consciousness and existence.

The seeker learns the art of lucid dreaming, where they become aware they are dreaming and can influence the course of their dreams. This practice is exhilarating and illuminating, providing a direct means of interacting with the subconscious mind. The seeker gains insights into their deepest fears, desires, and untapped potential through lucid dreaming.

In exploring dreams, the seeker also encounters archetypal symbols and themes. These archetypes, common across various cultures and times, speak to the universal aspects of the human experience. The seeker learns to interpret these symbols, understanding how they reflect their life journey and collective human challenges.

The realm of dreams becomes a space for healing and transformation. In dreams, the seeker confronts unresolved issues, processes emotional experiences, and works through psychological conflicts. This healing process often manifests as a greater sense of wholeness and well-being in waking life.

Dreams also serve as a creative wellspring. Many seekers find their most inventive ideas and inspirations come to them in dreams. Artists, writers, scientists, and inventors have long tapped into the dream world for innovative concepts and solutions to complex problems.

The seeker finds that their spiritual and personal growth is reflected in their dreams. As they evolve, so do their dreams. They begin to notice patterns and themes correlating with their waking life experiences and spiritual understandings, making dreams valuable tools for self-reflection and assessment.

In delving into "The Silence of the Cosmos," the seeker embarks on a profound journey to connect with the serenity and vastness of the universe. This exploration goes beyond physical silence, venturing into the cosmic stillness where profound peace and wisdom reside. The seeker learns that this cosmic silence is not emptiness but a rich tapestry of potentiality and presence, offering deep insights into the nature of existence.

The journey begins with an understanding that the cosmos, in its immense expanse, holds an ancient and profound silence. The seeker contemplates the stars, the galaxies, and the endless space, realizing that this cosmic quietude reflects the silence within. In this realization, they find a connection to the universe that is profoundly spiritual and grounding.

In embracing the cosmic silence, the seeker learns to quiet the mind and open the heart. This practice goes beyond the absence of sound; it is about tuning into the frequency of the universe. In this attunement, the seeker finds a sense of harmony and alignment with the cosmic rhythms, feeling at one with the vastness surrounding them.

The seeker discovers that the cosmic silence is a source of great wisdom and inspiration. It speaks in a language without words, communicating through intuition, synchronicities, and the subtle language of the soul. This communication is profound and transformative, guiding the seeker's spiritual journey.

Meditation becomes a pathway to experiencing cosmic silence. In meditation, the seeker transcends the confines of their self, reaching into the expansive quiet of the cosmos. These moments of deep connection bring insights and revelations that illuminate the seeker's path and purpose.

The cosmic silence teaches the seeker about the interconnectedness of all things. They realize that everything in the universe, from the smallest particle to the vastest galaxy, is part of a grand, interconnected web. This understanding fosters a deep sense of unity and compassion for all life forms.

In the stillness of the cosmos, the seeker confronts the concept of infinity and eternity. They grapple with the immensity of a universe that is both timeless and boundless. This confrontation is not frightening but awe-inspiring, expanding the seeker's mind and spirit.

The cosmic silence also serves as a reminder of the transient nature of human existence. Against the eternal cosmos, the seeker gains a new perspective on life's challenges and worries. They find peace and acceptance in the face of life's impermanence.

The seeker finds that the cosmic silence is a sanctuary, a place of refuge from the chaos and noise of the world. In this celestial calm, they discover solace and renewal, recharging their spiritual and emotional batteries. This sanctuary is always accessible, a constant source of comfort and inspiration.

Finally, the seeker understands that connecting with the cosmic silence is an ongoing journey. Each experience of this profound stillness brings deeper understanding and connection. By embracing the silence of the cosmos, the seeker taps into a wellspring of wisdom and peace, enriching their spiritual journey and bringing a celestial serenity to their daily life.

In the pursuit of "Understanding the Language of Silence," the seeker delves into the profound practice of deciphering the unspoken, the unheard, and the unseen. This journey is about realizing that silence is not an absence of communication but a different mode of understanding, rich with meaning and wisdom. The seeker learns that silence has its language, one that speaks directly to the heart and soul, conveying truths that words often fail to capture.

The journey begins with an appreciation for the nuances of silence. The seeker discovers that silence can express many meanings - peace, contemplation, sadness, awe, and more. They learn to listen to the subtle inflections of silence, understanding that it can communicate more profoundly than words.

In embracing silence, the seeker explores the space between words, finding that this space is often where the essence of communication lies. They realize that what is left unsaid can be as important as what is spoken. This understanding deepens their communication with others, making them more attuned to unspoken messages and emotions.

The seeker finds that silence is a powerful tool for self-reflection. In moments of quiet, they can hear their inner voice more clearly. This inner dialogue, free from external noise distraction, allows for deeper introspection and self-discovery.

Meditation becomes a fundamental practice in understanding the language of silence. Through meditation, the seeker learns to quiet the mind and listen to the stillness within. In this stillness, they find insights and wisdom that are not accessible amidst the clamor of daily life.

The seeker discovers the transformative power of silence. They find that periods of silence can facilitate healing, creativity, and spiritual growth. Silence catalyzes change, helping them process experiences, generate new ideas, and connect with their spiritual self.

In exploring the language of silence, the seeker learns about the balance between speaking and listening. They understand that effective communication involves expressing one's thoughts and being a receptive listener. This balance fosters more meaningful and authentic interactions.

The seeker finds that silence can bridge the gap between different cultures and beliefs. In silence, the barriers of language and ideology diminish, revealing the common humanity that lies beneath. This realization fosters a sense of unity and understanding with others.

Silence also teaches the seeker about the rhythm and timing of communication. They learn that there is a time to speak and be silent and that discerning the right moment is crucial for effective communication. This awareness enhances their interactions, making them more considerate and impactful.

Lastly, the seeker understands that learning the language of silence is a lifelong journey. It requires patience, attentiveness, and an open heart. As they continue to explore and understand silence, they find it becoming a profound part of their spiritual practice, enriching their life with depth, clarity, and a profound sense of connection to the world around them.

In addition to personal insights, dreams can also offer glimpses into the collective unconscious. The seeker might experience dreams connecting them with broader human concerns, global events, or ancestral memories. These experiences expand the seeker's awareness and sense of connection with the larger human community.

Finally, the seeker realizes that exploring the realm of dreams is an ongoing, ever-evolving journey. Each dream offers a unique opportunity for insight, growth, and exploration. By embracing the mysterious and often enigmatic nature of dreams, the seeker deepens their understanding of themselves and the universe, weaving the wisdom of the night into the tapestry of their daily life.

Chapter 4

In "Rediscovering Ancient Wisdom," the seeker embarks on a journey to reconnect with past civilizations and cultures' timeless truths and teachings. This exploration is about acquiring historical knowledge and understanding and integrating the profound spiritual insights that our ancestors have left behind. The seeker recognizes that ancient wisdom offers keys to comprehending the universe, life, and the self, transcending time and place.

The journey begins with the realization that ancient wisdom is not obsolete or irrelevant but is as applicable today as it was centuries ago. The seeker delves into the study of sacred texts, myths, and teachings from various traditions, discovering universal truths that resonate deeply with their own experiences and beliefs.

In rediscovering these ancient teachings, the seeker finds they offer insights into the nature of existence, the cosmos, and the human spirit. These teachings guide living a life of balance, purpose, and harmony. The seeker learns to see these ancient philosophies not as mere historical artifacts but as living, breathing wisdom.

The seeker explores the practices and rituals of ancient cultures, understanding that these were not just religious or ceremonial acts but ways of connecting with deeper realities. They experiment with these practices, finding that they offer profound experiences of connection, transformation, and enlightenment.

In this journey, the seeker also recognizes the interconnectedness of all wisdom traditions. They see the threads that connect the teachings of the East and the West, the North and the South, realizing that, at their core, all traditions speak of similar truths and aspirations.

The ancient wisdom teaches the seeker about the cycles of nature, the rhythms of the universe, and the laws of life. These teachings foster a more profound respect for the natural world and a greater understanding of the seeker's place within the cosmic order.

The seeker learns to appreciate the symbolism and allegory used in ancient teachings. They understand that these symbolic languages convey complex spiritual truths in ways that transcend words and rational thought. This symbolism becomes a key to unlocking deeper layers of meaning and understanding.

In embracing ancient wisdom, the seeker finds guidance for personal growth and self-realization. These teachings provide a roadmap for spiritual development, offering insights into overcoming challenges, achieving inner peace, and realizing one's true potential.

The seeker discovers that ancient wisdom offers insights into community, relationships, and social harmony. These teachings provide principles for living together in peace, respect, and mutual support, fostering a sense of global kinship and interconnectedness.

Lastly, the seeker realizes that rediscovering ancient wisdom is an ongoing process. Each reading, each practice, and each reflection brings new insights and deeper understandings. By reconnecting with the knowledge of the past, the seeker weaves these timeless truths into the fabric of their daily life, enriching their journey with depth, clarity, and a profound sense of connection to the ages.

In "The Teachings of Timeless Myths," the seeker explores the profound spiritual and life lessons hidden within ancient myths and legends. This exploration is a study of old tales and a deep dive into the universal truths and human experiences they encapsulate. The seeker realizes that myths, irrespective of their cultural origins, hold timeless wisdom, offering insights into the human condition and the mysteries of existence.

The journey begins with an understanding that myths are more than just stories; they are symbolic narratives that reflect humanity's most profound questions and truths. The seeker delves into myths from various cultures, finding common themes of creation, transformation, heroism, and the eternal struggle between good and evil. These themes resonate with their own life experiences and spiritual quests.

In these ancient myths, the seeker finds reflections of their journey. Heroes and heroines, gods and goddesses, monsters and mentors – all these characters represent different aspects of the human psyche and the spiritual path. The seeker learns to identify with these archetypes, understanding their relevance in their own life.

The teachings of these myths extend to understanding the cycles of nature and the universe. Myths often depict cycles of birth, death, and rebirth, mirroring the natural cycles of the world and the existential cycles of the human experience. The seeker gains a deeper appreciation for the rhythm of life and the transformative process of growth and renewal.

Myths also teach the power of facing and overcoming challenges. Just as heroes embark on quests and face trials, the seeker understands that their life challenges are opportunities for growth and self-discovery. These stories inspire courage and resilience, reminding the seeker of their inner strength and potential.

In exploring timeless myths, the seeker discovers the art of deciphering symbols and allegories. They learn that every element in a myth – a character, an object, a journey – carries a deeper meaning. This symbolic language opens up new layers of understanding and insight into the human experience and the spiritual journey.

The seeker finds that myths guide ethical and moral dilemmas. Through the actions and fates of mythical characters, the seeker contemplates virtues like bravery, wisdom, compassion, and integrity. These stories offer moral compasses, guiding the seeker in making choices aligned with their values and principles.

Myths also offer a window into understanding the collective unconscious. The seeker realizes these stories are not just individual creations but emerge from the shared human psyche. This realization fosters a sense of connection with humanity across time and space, bridging cultural and temporal divides.

The exploration of myths becomes a source of creativity and imagination for the seeker. These stories stimulate the mind, inspiring new ideas, perspectives, and visions. With its rich imagery and narrative, the mythical world becomes a wellspring of inspiration for the seeker's life and creative expression.

Finally, the seeker understands that the teachings of timeless myths are an ongoing source of wisdom and learning. Each revisiting of a myth can reveal new insights and revelations, mirroring the seeker's growth and evolving understanding. The seeker enriches their journey by weaving the wisdom of ancient myths into their life, finding guidance, inspiration, and a deeper connection to the universal human story.

In "Embracing the Sacred Rituals," the seeker ventures into the realm of ancient and contemporary practices that connect the physical to the metaphysical, the mundane to the divine. This exploration is about recognizing and participating in rituals that transcend time, bridging the earthly and the spiritual realms. The seeker discovers that these sacred acts, rooted in intention and symbolism, offer profound pathways to transformation and enlightenment.

The journey begins with an understanding that simple or elaborate rituals are imbued with meaning and purpose. The seeker learns to see the sacred in everyday actions by infusing them with mindfulness and intention. This shift transforms mundane activities into holy rituals, elevating the seeker's daily life into a living, breathing practice of spirituality.

In delving into ancient rituals, the seeker uncovers the wisdom of ancestral traditions. They explore ceremonies and rites from diverse cultures, finding common threads of connection, reverence, and communion with the divine. These ancient practices reveal the universal human desire to connect with something greater than oneself, offering the seeker a tapestry of spiritual heritage to draw upon.

The seeker discovers the power of ritual in creating and marking sacred space and time. They learn that rituals can sanctify moments, places, and transitions, providing a framework for experiencing the holy in the present moment. This sanctification brings depth and richness to the seeker's life experience, turning the ordinary into the extraordinary.

Rituals become a means of personal and communal expression for the seeker. They understand that through ritual, individuals and communities articulate their values, beliefs, and aspirations. Participating in or creating rituals allows the seeker to express their spiritual journey in tangible forms, fostering a sense of belonging and shared purpose.

The seeker finds that rituals are about tradition, personalization, and evolution. They experiment with adapting ancient rituals and creating new ones that resonate with their journey. This creative engagement with ritual allows the seeker to craft significant practices that reflect their unique path.

In embracing sacred rituals, the seeker experiences the transformative power of symbolic actions. Through their symbolic language, they realize that rituals can facilitate profound changes in consciousness, leading to healing, growth, and transformation. This symbolic engagement offers a direct experience of the spiritual truths that rituals embody.

The seeker learns the importance of intention in rituals. They understand that the power of a ritual lies not in its external form but in the purpose behind it.

In "The Path of Symbology and Archetypes," the seeker explores the universal symbols and archetypal figures that inhabit the collective unconscious. This journey is not merely an academic study but a profound engagement with the timeless patterns and images that shape human experience and consciousness. The seeker discovers that these symbols and archetypes are keys to unlocking profound spiritual truths and understanding the interconnectedness of all life.

The journey begins with an understanding of symbols as the language of the soul. The seeker learns that symbols transcend ordinary language, conveying meanings that are multi-layered and rich with significance. Through symbols, the seeker taps into a deeper level of awareness, where complex spiritual truths can be intuitively grasped and internalized.

In delving into archetypes, the seeker encounters the foundational characters and themes that recur across cultures and epochs. Figures like the Hero, the Wise Old Man, the Great Mother, and the Trickster become familiar guides on the spiritual journey. The seeker realizes that these archetypes represent aspects of their psyche, offering insights into their personal growth and challenges.

The seeker finds that engaging with symbology and archetypes is a dynamic process. As they delve deeper, they discover that these symbols and figures evolve in meaning and relevance. This evolution reflects the seeker's growth and changing understanding, making the engagement with symbology and archetypes a profoundly personal and transformative experience.

Symbols and archetypes serve as bridges between the conscious and unconscious mind. The seeker learns to navigate this interface, uncovering hidden fears, desires, and wisdom in their unconscious's shadowy realms. This exploration brings to light aspects of the self that are often overlooked or suppressed, facilitating healing and integration.

The natural world becomes a rich source of symbols and archetypes for the seeker. They begin to see the symbolic significance in the cycles of the moon, the changing seasons, and the myriad forms of plant and animal life. This connection deepens their sense of unity with nature and the cosmos, revealing the sacredness embedded in the fabric of everyday life.

The seeker also explores the role of symbology and archetypes in art, literature, and mythology. They find that creative expressions are replete with symbolic imagery and archetypal themes, serving as mirrors to the human psyche and the spiritual journey. Engaging with these artistic and literary works becomes a way of engaging with humanity's collective dreams and aspirations.

In meditation and visualization, the seeker uses symbols and archetypes as focal points for contemplation. These practices allow the seeker to internalize the energies and lessons of specific symbols and archetypes, facilitating personal transformation and spiritual awakening.

The seeker learns to create their own symbolic language and personal mythology. They craft a deeply personal and universally connected narrative by identifying and working with symbols and archetypes that resonate with their unique journey. This creative act becomes a powerful tool for self-expression and spiritual exploration.

Finally, the seeker recognizes that the path of symbology and archetypes is endless and ever-unfolding. Each symbol and archetype is a doorway to deeper understanding and connection. By continuously engaging with these universal patterns, the seeker weaves a rich tapestry of meaning and purpose, enriching their journey with the wisdom of the ages and the collective insights of humanity.

In "The Labyrinth of Self-Discovery," the seeker embarks on a profound journey within, navigating the intricate pathways of their psyche. This exploration is a quest to uncover the true essence of the self beyond the layers of social conditioning, personal history, and ego. The seeker learns this internal labyrinth is not a maze to escape from but a sacred space to journey through, offering invaluable insights and revelations about their true nature and purpose.

The journey begins with the recognition that the labyrinth of self-discovery is both complex and richly rewarding. The seeker understands that each turn and twist presents an opportunity for deeper self-awareness and transformation. They approach this inner journey with reverence and openness, ready to encounter the myriad aspects of their being.

In navigating this labyrinth, the seeker encounters their shadows – the parts of themselves that have been ignored, repressed, or denied. Rather than fearing these shadow aspects, the seeker learns to embrace them with compassion and understanding. This integration of the shadow brings about a more complete and authentic sense of self.

The seeker discovers that the labyrinth is filled with mirrors reflecting their fears, desires, and the multitude of selves they embody. These reflections challenge the seeker to confront their illusions and misconceptions about who they are. Through this confrontation, the seeker gains clarity and moves closer to their essence.

Symbols and signposts appear along the path, guiding the seeker through the labyrinth. These symbols, unique to each individual's journey, offer clues and insights that aid navigation. The seeker learns to interpret these signs, understanding that they are messages from their deeper self.

Moments of stillness and solitude within the labyrinth become sacred pauses, allowing the seeker to absorb the lessons and insights gained. These pauses are essential, providing space for reflection, integration, and preparation for the next phase of the journey.

The labyrinth reveals the interconnectedness of all aspects of the seeker's life. Relationships, challenges, and experiences are interconnected pathways within the maze, each contributing to the seeker's growth and self-discovery. This holistic view fosters a deeper understanding of the self and the journey.

At the labyrinth's heart, the seeker encounters their essence, the unchanging core of their being. This encounter is a profound moment of realization, where the seeker experiences a deep sense of unity with themselves and the universe. It is a moment of awakening to their true nature and potential.

The journey through the labyrinth is cyclical, not linear. The seeker understands that self-discovery is an ongoing process, with each journey through the maze offering more profound layers of insight and understanding. This cyclical nature reflects the continuous growth and evolution of the self.

Finally, the seeker emerges from the labyrinth transformed. They carry the wisdom, strength, and clarity gained from the journey. This transformation is not an end but a new beginning, with the seeker now equipped to live with greater authenticity, purpose, and connection to their true self. With its challenges and revelations, the labyrinth of self-discovery becomes a cherished part of the seeker's spiritual journey, enriching their life with profound depth and meaning.

In "The Alchemy of Inner Transformation," the seeker embarks on a profound process of metamorphosis, turning the base elements of their being into spiritual gold. This journey is about embracing the transformative power within, utilizing life's challenges and experiences as catalysts for profound change. The seeker learns that true alchemy is not about external changes but about the transmutation of the soul, leading to enlightenment and self-realization.

The journey begins with an understanding that the raw materials for this alchemical process are the seeker's experiences, emotions, and thoughts. The seeker recognizes that even the most challenging situations hold the potential for growth and transformation. They approach these experiences with curiosity and openness, ready to extract the wisdom and strength they offer.

In navigating the alchemy of inner transformation, the seeker discovers the importance of embracing their shadows. They learn that by confronting and integrating the darker aspects of themselves, they can achieve a more profound sense of wholeness and balance. This integration is a critical alchemical process, turning leaden fears and weaknesses into golden insights and virtues.

The seeker finds that the fire of transformation is fueled by intention and will. They understand that a clear and focused intention sets the direction for their alchemical journey, while their will provides the energy to sustain the process. This combination of intention and willpower becomes the flame that transmutes the base elements of their being.

Symbols and archetypes play a crucial role in the alchemy of inner transformation. The seeker learns to work with these powerful symbols, drawing upon their energy and wisdom to facilitate their metamorphosis. These symbols serve as guides and tools, helping the seeker navigate the complex processes of alchemical change.

The seeker discovers that alchemy involves a delicate balance between action and surrender. They learn the art of taking purposeful action toward their transformation while surrendering to the larger forces at work. This balance allows the seeker to co-create their metamorphosis with the universe, harmonizing their efforts with the flow of divine energy.

The alchemical process teaches the seeker about the interconnectedness of all aspects of their life. They realize that transformation in one area inevitably impacts others, leading to a holistic change. This understanding encourages the seeker to embrace the alchemy of inner transformation in all facets of their being, from the physical to the spiritual.

In the crucible of inner alchemy, the seeker experiences moments of dissolution, where old identities and beliefs are melted away. These moments, though challenging, are essential for creating space for the new. The seeker learns to trust the process, knowing that a more authentic and empowered self will emerge from this dissolution.

The journey of inner alchemy is marked by cycles of death and rebirth. The seeker understands that each cycle is an opportunity for renewal and growth. They embrace these cycles, recognizing that each rebirth brings them closer to their true essence and higher self.

Finally, the seeker realizes that the alchemy of inner transformation is an ongoing journey without a definitive end. Each stage of transformation opens the door to new levels of awareness and being. By committing to the path of alchemical change, the seeker continually evolves, becoming a living embodiment of spiritual alchemy, radiating the light of their transformed self into the world.

In "The Harmony of Universal Laws," the seeker embarks on an enlightening journey to understand and align with the fundamental principles that govern existence. This exploration delves into the mystical and scientific realms, revealing that the universe operates on immutable laws that maintain balance and order. The seeker learns that living in harmony with these laws can achieve a more profound sense of coherence with the cosmos, leading to a life of greater ease, purpose, and fulfillment.

The journey begins with recognizing the Law of Correspondence, "As above, so below; as within, so without." The seeker contemplates this principle, realizing that the universe's macrocosm is reflected in the microcosm of their being. This understanding fosters a profound connection with the cosmos, guiding the seeker to live in a way that reflects the harmony and order of the universe.

The seeker explores the Law of Vibration, understanding that everything in the universe, from the smallest particle to the vastest galaxy, is in constant motion, vibrating at different frequencies. They learn to attune their vibrational frequency through thoughts, emotions, and actions, resonating with the energies that promote peace, joy, and love.

Through the Law of Cause and Effect, the seeker realizes that every action has a corresponding reaction. This law teaches them the importance of mindfulness and responsibility in their choices and actions, knowing that what they put into the universe will inevitably return to them. This understanding encourages the seeker to act with integrity and compassion.

The seeker delves into the Law of Attraction, discovering that like attracts like. They understand that focusing their thoughts and energies on what they wish to manifest can attract corresponding experiences and opportunities. This law empowers the seeker to co-create their reality with the universe, aligning their desires with the highest good.

The Law of Rhythm becomes a dance the seeker learns to flow with. They recognize the cyclical nature of life and the universe, embracing the natural ebbs and flows of existence. This alignment with the rhythmic cycles brings a sense of grace and ease to the seeker's journey, allowing them to move with the tides of life rather than against them.

The seeker contemplates the Law of Polarity, understanding that everything has its opposite, and these opposites are two extremes of the same thing. This law teaches the seeker to find balance and harmony within the dualities of life, transcending the polarities to find a unifying middle path.

Through the Law of Gender, the seeker explores the masculine and feminine energies within themselves and the universe. They learn to balance these energies, recognizing that both are essential for creation, growth, and harmony. This balance fosters wholeness and integration within the seeker's being.

The Law of Perpetual Transmutation of Energy reveals to the seeker the dynamic potential for change inherent in the universe. They learn that energy is constantly flowing and transforming, and by directing their focus and intention, they can influence these energetic transformations in their lives and environments.

In embracing these universal laws, the seeker finds a roadmap for living in alignment with the universe's natural order. They understand that these laws are not constraints but guiding principles that, when honored, lead to a life of harmony, abundance, and fulfillment.

Finally, the seeker realizes that the harmony of universal laws is an ongoing discovery. Each day presents new opportunities to deepen their understanding and alignment with these principles. By following these laws, the seeker becomes a co-creator with the universe, participating in the majestic symphony of existence with awareness, intention, and joy.

In "The Voyage of Cosmic Connection," the seeker embarks on an awe-inspiring journey to deepen their bond with the universe. This exploration transcends the physical dimensions, venturing into the realms of energy, spirit, and the interconnected web of all existence. The seeker discovers that every element of the cosmos, from the smallest particle to the grandest galaxy, is intricately linked in a dance of unity and harmony.

The journey begins with the awakening to the realization that the universe is alive and conscious. The seeker perceives the cosmos not as an inanimate expanse but as a vibrant, conscious entity with which they can interact and communicate. This profound understanding transforms the seeker's relationship with the universe, inviting a dialogue with the cosmos.

In forging this cosmic connection, the seeker learns to attune to the frequencies of the universe. They understand that by aligning their vibrational energy with that of the cosmos, they can achieve a resonance that facilitates a deeper communion with the universal consciousness. This attunement opens doorways to wisdom, guidance, and insights inaccessible through ordinary means.

The seeker discovers the power of intention in navigating this cosmic voyage. They realize that their thoughts, desires, and intentions are powerful forces that interact with the fabric of the universe. By setting clear, heartfelt intentions, the seeker sends ripples through the cosmos, drawing towards them the energies and experiences that resonate with their deepest aspirations.

The vastness of space becomes a mirror for the seeker's inner space. They explore the parallels between the outer universe and their inner world, recognizing that the macrocosm of the cosmos is reflected in the microcosm of their being. This mirroring reveals the unity of all existence, showing the seeker that they are also delving into the depths of their soul by exploring the universe.

The seeker learns to navigate the cosmic currents through meditation and contemplation. These practices become celestial voyages, where the seeker transcends the physical boundaries of time and space, journeying into the heart of the cosmos. In these meditative states, the seeker experiences oneness with the universe, basking in the profound peace and love that pervades all creation.

The cosmic connection teaches the seeker about the flow of synchronicities. They begin to notice meaningful coincidences and serendipitous events that seem to guide their path. The seeker understands that these synchronicities are signs from the universe, confirming their alignment with the cosmic flow and guiding their journey.

In this voyage, the seeker encounters the beauty of cosmic cycles and rhythms. They observe the orderly patterns of planets, stars, and galaxies, recognizing these celestial movements as expressions of the cosmic dance. This awareness of cosmic rhythms enhances the seeker's understanding of the cyclical nature of their own life and the interconnectedness of all things.

The seeker finds solace and strength in the cosmic connection during times of challenge and change. They learn to draw upon the vast reservoirs of energy and support available in the universe, finding comfort in the knowledge that they are never alone but always supported by the cosmic web of life.

Finally, the seeker realizes that the voyage of cosmic connection is an eternal journey. There is no final destination, for the universe and the seeker's relationship is ever-expanding. Each moment of connection deepens their bond with the cosmos, infusing their life with a sense of wonder, gratitude, and unity. By embracing the cosmic connection, the seeker weaves their thread into the grand tapestry of existence, participating in the magnificent symphony of the universe with awareness, reverence, and love.

In "The Journey Through Sacred Geometry," the seeker explores the fundamental patterns and shapes that form the universe's building blocks. This journey is a profound engagement with the mathematical harmony and beauty underlying all creation. The seeker discovers that sacred geometry is not merely a subject of intellectual study but a pathway to experiencing the divine order and interconnectedness of existence.

The journey begins with understanding the basic shapes and patterns that recur throughout nature and the cosmos. The seeker learns about the significance of the circle, the spiral, the hexagon, and other geometric forms that appear in everything from the structure of galaxies to the spirals of seashells. This recognition of recurring patterns awakens a sense of wonder and a deeper appreciation for the natural world.

In delving into the principles of sacred geometry, the seeker uncovers the profound symbolism embedded in these patterns. They explore the meaning behind the Flower of Life, the Fibonacci sequence, the Platonic solids, and other geometric symbols, discovering that these shapes hold keys to understanding the mysteries of creation and the essence of life itself.

The seeker finds that sacred geometry offers insights into the fabric of space and time. They contemplate the geometric structure of the universe, from the vast arrangement of celestial bodies to the intricate designs of subatomic particles. This exploration reveals the inherent order and harmony that pervade the cosmos, reflecting a grand, unified design.

Sacred geometry becomes a meditative tool for the seeker. They engage with geometric patterns through drawing, visualization, and contemplation, finding that these practices enhance their concentration, intuition, and spiritual awareness. Creating and meditating upon geometric forms becomes a sacred act, connecting the seeker with the underlying unity of all things.

The seeker learns to apply the principles of sacred geometry in their environment. They explore geometric patterns in architecture, art, and design, understanding how these shapes influence energy flow, aesthetics, and consciousness. This application of sacred geometry enhances the harmony and sacredness of their living spaces and creative expressions.

In healing and well-being, the seeker discovers the therapeutic applications of sacred geometry. They explore how geometric shapes and patterns balance energy, promote healing, and support physical and emotional health. This understanding adds a new dimension to their approach to wellness, integrating the healing power of sacred patterns.

The seeker realizes that sacred geometry is a language that transcends cultural and temporal boundaries. They explore the use of geometric patterns in spiritual traditions worldwide, finding commonalities that point to a universal understanding of these sacred forms. This exploration fosters a sense of unity and interconnectedness with diverse cultures and spiritual paths.

Sacred geometry deepens the seeker's understanding of the creative process. They see artistic and creative endeavors as reflections of the cosmic creative force, with geometry as a bridge between the visible and invisible realms. This insight infuses their creative work with a sense of purpose and connection to the larger cosmic order.

Finally, the seeker recognizes that the journey through sacred geometry is an endless exploration of the divine blueprint of creation. Each geometric pattern and each mathematical ratio is a portal to more profound wisdom and spiritual insight. By studying and integrating sacred geometry into their life, the seeker aligns themselves with the fundamental harmony of the universe, weaving the holy patterns of creation into the tapestry of their spiritual journey.

In "The Quest for Universal Harmony," the seeker embarks on a profound journey to align their spirit with the symphony of the cosmos. This exploration delves into the intricate dance of energies, frequencies, and vibrations that constitute the fabric of the universe. The seeker discovers that by attuning themselves to this cosmic harmony, they can experience a profound sense of unity and peace, transcending the discord of everyday life.

The journey begins with recognizing the universe as a vast, interconnected web of vibrations. The seeker learns everything, from the smallest particle to the grandest galaxy, which vibrates at its unique frequency. This understanding fosters a deep appreciation for the delicate balance and order that govern the cosmos, inspiring the seeker to find this harmonic resonance within themselves.

In seeking universal harmony, the seeker becomes attuned to the music of the spheres, the ancient concept that posits the movements of celestial bodies as a form of musical harmony. They listen for the subtle, celestial melodies that orchestrate the dance of the planets and stars, finding in these cosmic rhythms a reflection of their inner harmony.

The seeker explores the concept of resonance, understanding that by vibrating in harmony with positive frequencies, they can elevate their vibrational state. They engage in practices like meditation, chanting, and sound healing, using these tools to align their energy with the vibrations of love, peace, and enlightenment.

The quest leads the seeker to discover the power of intention and thought. They realize that thoughts and intentions are not merely abstract concepts but vibrational energies that can influence the physical and spiritual realms. By cultivating positive, harmonious thoughts, the seeker contributes to universal harmony, weaving their intentions into the cosmic tapestry.

The seeker finds guidance in the natural world, observing how nature operates in balance and harmony. They learn from the rhythms of the seasons, the cycles of growth and decay, and the symbiotic relationships between species. This immersion in nature's harmony teaches the seeker about the interconnectedness of all life and the importance of living under natural laws.

In their quest, the seeker encounters the principle of synchronicity, experiencing meaningful coincidences that signal alignment with the universal flow. These synchronicities serve as affirmations from the universe, encouraging the seeker on their path toward harmony and reinforcing their sense of connection with the cosmic order.

The seeker delves into the wisdom of ancient spiritual traditions, which teach about the balance of yin and yang, the middle way, and the path of dharma. These teachings offer valuable insights into achieving harmony within and without, guiding the seeker toward a life of balance, compassion, and mindfulness.

Through their quest for universal harmony, the seeker experiences moments of profound unity with all existence. In these transcendent moments, the boundaries between self and other dissolve, revealing the underlying oneness of the universe. These experiences of unity bring deep joy, peace, and a sense of belonging to the seeker.

Finally, the seeker realizes that the quest for universal harmony is a continuous journey, an ever-unfolding process of learning, growing, and attuning to the deeper rhythms of existence. They understand that harmony is not a static state but a dynamic equilibrium, requiring constant awareness and adjustment. By embracing this quest, the seeker becomes a co-creator of harmony, contributing their unique melody to the grand symphony of the cosmos.

Chapter 5

In "Cultivating Inner Peace," the seeker embarks on a transformative journey to nurture profound tranquility and serenity within their being. This quest is not merely about escaping the chaos of the external world but about discovering a wellspring of peace that resides at the core of their essence. The seeker learns that inner peace is a sanctuary they can carry within themselves, offering solace and stability amidst life's storms.

The journey begins with the realization that inner peace is an innate state, obscured only by the turbulence of thoughts, emotions, and external circumstances. The seeker understands that uncovering this peace requires a gentle but persistent excavation of the layers of unrest that have accumulated over time. They approach this task with patience and compassion, knowing that each layer removed brings them closer to their authentic, peaceful nature.

In cultivating inner peace, the seeker adopts practices of mindfulness and meditation. These practices become sacred rituals that quiet the mind, soothe the soul, and anchor the seeker in the present moment. Through consistent engagement, the seeker finds that the waves of anxiety, fear, and discord begin to subside, revealing the calm waters of inner peace beneath.

The seeker learns the art of acceptance and surrender, understanding that resistance to what is often the source of turmoil. By embracing the present moment, with all its imperfections and uncertainties, the seeker allows peace to emerge naturally. This acceptance does not mean passivity but acknowledging the present as the foundation upon which change can be built.

In their quest for inner peace, the seeker explores the power of forgiveness. They discover that holding onto grievances, resentment, and anger binds them to the past and obstructs their path to peace.

Through forgiveness, the seeker releases these bonds, freeing themselves and others and opening the way for healing and tranquility.

The seeker finds that inner peace is intricately connected to self-love and compassion. They learn to treat themselves with the same kindness and understanding they would offer a dear friend. This self-compassion becomes a balm for the soul, healing old wounds and fostering a gentle, peaceful relationship with oneself.

Nature becomes a profound teacher in the seeker's quest for inner peace. They find solace in the beauty and stillness of the natural world, which reflects and reinforces their inner tranquility. Time spent in nature becomes vital, recharging their spirit and reminding them of the peace that pervades all creation.

The seeker understands that inner peace is not a destination but a journey. It requires daily nurturing, a commitment to practices that foster tranquility, and a vigilant return to peace when life's challenges and distractions arise. This ongoing commitment becomes a source of strength and resilience, enabling the seeker to maintain their inner sanctuary regardless of external conditions.

In cultivating inner peace, the seeker becomes a beacon of peace for others. Their tranquil presence has a calming effect on those around them, creating ripples of serenity that extend into their relationships, communities, and beyond. The seeker realizes that by nurturing their inner peace, they contribute to creating a more peaceful world.

Finally, the seeker recognizes that inner peace is a profound act of faith and trust. It involves a deep trust in life's journey, the unfolding of each moment, and the inherent goodness that lies within and all around. By cultivating inner peace, the seeker affirms their trust in the universe, embracing life with an open heart and a tranquil spirit, ready to meet each moment with grace and composure.

In "The Practice of Mindful Living," the seeker embarks on a transformative journey to infuse each moment with awareness and presence. This exploration is about transcending the automatic pilot of daily routines and awakening to the richness of life as it unfolds. The seeker discovers that mindful living is an art, turning mundane activities into sacred rituals and ordinary experiences into profound lessons.

The journey begins with the realization that each moment holds a universe of possibilities and that awareness is the key to unlocking them. The seeker learns to slow down and observe the nuances of their thoughts, emotions, and sensations, finding a doorway to a more profound connection with the self and the world in this observation.

In cultivating mindfulness, the seeker adopts practices that anchor them in the present. They learn to breathe with intention, to savor each bite of food, to listen with full attention, and to observe their surroundings with fresh eyes. These practices transform everyday experiences, revealing the beauty and wonder that often go unnoticed.

The seeker discovers the power of mindfulness in transforming relationships. By being fully present with others, the seeker fosters deeper connections and understanding. Mindful listening becomes a gift they offer, creating space for authentic communication and shared humanity.

In the realm of challenges and difficulties, the seeker finds mindfulness a sanctuary of calm. They learn to face stress, fear, and pain with a centered presence, allowing these experiences to be felt fully and released. This mindful approach to challenges fosters resilience, compassion, and a more profound sense of peace.

The practice of mindful living extends to the seeker's interaction with nature. They find that by being present with the natural world, they can sense the intricate web of life and their place within it. This connection deepens their appreciation for the planet and inspires a commitment to living harmoniously with the environment.

The seeker realizes that mindfulness is not confined to meditation cushions or quiet spaces but can be woven into the fabric of daily life. From washing dishes to walking to work, every act becomes an opportunity for mindfulness, turning routine tasks into moments of joy and discovery.

Mindful living teaches the seeker about the impermanence of all things. By observing the constant flow of life, the seeker understands that change is the only constant. This understanding cultivates a sense of detachment and freedom, allowing the seeker to gracefully embrace life's transitory nature.

In their quest for mindful living, the seeker encounters the challenge of distraction and the pull of past and future concerns. They learn techniques to gently guide their attention back to the present, understanding that mindfulness is a practice of continual return, a dance of presence amidst the distractions of life.

Finally, the seeker recognizes mindful living is a path of endless discovery. Each day offers new landscapes of experience to explore with awareness, each moment a fresh canvas on which to practice the art of presence. By committing to mindful living, the seeker transforms their life into a living meditation, a journey of awakening to the wonder and beauty of existence, moment by moment.

Chapter 6:

In "Embracing the Eternal Now," the seeker embarks on a transformative journey to dwell fully in the present moment, transcending the constraints of the past and future. This exploration delves into the essence of timelessness, where the seeker discovers the profound peace and clarity that arise from being immersed in the now. The seeker learns that the eternal now is not just a concept but a living experience, offering a sanctuary of presence in the midst of life's flux.

The journey begins with the realization that the present moment is the only true reality, the only time where life truly unfolds. The seeker learns to release the burdens of past regrets and future anxieties, understanding that these are mere shadows that distract from the luminosity of the now. This liberation from time's hold brings a sense of freedom and lightness to the seeker's journey.

In cultivating a practice of presence, the seeker finds that mindfulness is key. They learn to anchor their awareness in the sensations, thoughts, and experiences that arise moment by moment. This mindful attention becomes a gateway to the eternal now, revealing the richness and depth of each instant that had previously gone unnoticed.

The seeker discovers that embracing the eternal now opens the heart to the beauty and wonder of life. They begin to see the miraculous in the ordinary, the sacred in the mundane. This shift in perception transforms their experience of the world, infusing their days with a sense of awe and reverence.

In the eternal now, the seeker finds a profound connection to their inner self. Freed from the distractions of past and future, they encounter the essence of their being with clarity and authenticity. This encounter with the self is both grounding and liberating, offering a steady compass in the journey of life.

The practice of being in the now teaches the seeker about the impermanence of all things. They learn to hold experiences lightly, cherishing them without clinging, knowing that each moment is a fleeting gift. This understanding fosters a graceful acceptance of life's ebb and flow, imbuing the seeker with a serene resilience.

The seeker realizes that the eternal now is a space of infinite potential. Without the constraints of past and future, each moment holds the possibility for new beginnings and transformations. This recognition empowers the seeker to act with intention and creativity, co-creating their reality with the universe.

Embracing the eternal now also deepens the seeker's relationships. By being fully present with others, they forge connections of depth and authenticity. These connections, rooted in the shared ground of the now, are sources of joy and companionship on the spiritual journey.

The seeker learns that the eternal now is not an escape from life's challenges but a way to meet them with clarity and strength. In the clarity of the present, solutions emerge, and difficulties are faced with courage. This presence becomes a source of inner strength, enabling the seeker to navigate life's storms with grace.

Finally, the seeker understands that embracing the eternal now is an ongoing practice, a continual return to the present whenever the mind wanders to past or future. By committing to this practice, the seeker cultivates a life of presence, experiencing the unfolding of each day with a heart full of peace and eyes wide open to the miracle of existence.

In "The Journey of Letting Go," the seeker embarks on a profound path of release and surrender, shedding the weights of attachments, expectations, and old identities. This exploration is a deep dive into the art of relinquishment, where the seeker discovers the liberation and renewal that come from letting go. The seeker learns that letting go is not a loss but a return to the essence, a clearing of space for new growth and possibilities.

The journey begins with the recognition of the burdens that the seeker has carried - the clinging to past hurts, the fear of future uncertainties, and the tight grip on self-imposed identities. The seeker understands that these burdens are barriers to freedom and growth, obscuring the light of their true nature.

In the process of letting go, the seeker encounters the challenge of attachment. They learn that attachment is rooted in the mind's desire for security and certainty. By observing and understanding these attachments, the seeker begins to loosen their hold, finding peace in uncertainty and security within themselves.

The seeker discovers the power of forgiveness as a key to letting go. They realize that forgiveness is not condoning hurt but freeing oneself from the chains of resentment. This act of forgiveness, both for others and oneself, becomes a liberating force, opening the heart to healing and renewal.

Letting go teaches the seeker about the fluidity of identity. They come to see themselves not as a fixed entity but as a dynamic being, ever-evolving and changing. This understanding allows them to release outdated self-concepts, embracing the unfolding journey of who they are becoming.

The practice of letting go leads the seeker to a deeper trust in the flow of life. They learn to surrenderto the wisdom of the universe, trusting that each release brings them closer to their highest path. This trust in the natural process of life and its inherent wisdom transforms fear into courage, guiding the seeker through the act of letting go with grace.

In embracing the journey of letting go, the seeker finds that space is created for newness to enter. They understand that every release is an invitation for fresh opportunities, relationships, and insights to blossom. This perspective turns the act of letting go into an act of making room for abundance and growth.

The seeker learns that letting go is also an act of self-love. By releasing what no longer serves them, they honor their well-being and respect their journey. This self-love reinforces the seeker's commitment to their growth, nurturing their spirit and propelling them forward on their path.

Letting go becomes a practice of mindfulness for the seeker. They become more aware of the present moment, unburdened by the past or the future. This mindfulness enhances their capacity to experience life fully, savoring each moment with a heart unencumbered by what they have let go.

The seeker discovers that the journey of letting go is intertwined with the journey of acceptance. Accepting the impermanence of all things, the fluidity of life, and the beauty of transformation makes letting go not just necessary but a natural and harmonious part of existence.

Finally, the seeker recognizes that letting go is a continuous journey, not a one-time event. Each day presents new opportunities to release, forgive, and surrender. By embracing this journey, the seeker cultivates a life of freedom, lightness, and openness, ready to receive the blessings that await in the space they have created through letting go.

In "The Path of Heart-Centered Living," the seeker ventures into the depths of their heart, exploring a way of life guided by love, compassion, and intuition. This exploration reveals that the heart is not just an organ of emotion but a profound source of wisdom and connection. The seeker learns that living from the heart opens doors to authentic relationships, creative expression, and a deep sense of alignment with the universe's rhythms.

The journey begins with the awakening to the heart's intelligence, an understanding that the heart has its own language and logic, distinct from the mind's analytical chatter. The seeker cultivates the ability to listen to this heart wisdom, finding guidance and clarity in its gentle nudges and expansive feelings.

In embracing heart-centered living, the seeker discovers the transformative power of love. They realize that love is the most potent force in the universe, capable of healing, uniting, and elevating. By centering their life around love, the seeker becomes a catalyst for positive change, radiating warmth and kindness wherever they go.

The seeker learns that heart-centered living involves vulnerability and openness. They allow themselves to be seen and known, embracing their true selves with all their strengths and weaknesses. This authenticity fosters deeper connections with others, built on trust and mutual respect.

The path of heart-centered living teaches the seeker about the balance between giving and receiving love. They understand that this balance is essential for well-being and growth. By opening their heart to receive love as freely as they give it, the seeker nurtures their spirit and strengthens their capacity to love.

The seeker finds that living from the heart enhances their intuition and creativity. The heart, with its connection to the deeper currents of life, becomes a wellspring of inspiration and insight. This connection empowers the seeker to create and live in ways that reflect their deepest values and visions.

Heart-centered living leads the seeker to cultivate compassion, both for themselves and for others. They learn to meet pain, suffering, and imperfection with a compassionate heart, offering understanding and support. This compassion becomes a healing balm, soothing wounds and mending divides.

The seeker discovers that the heart is a bridge to the divine, a sacred portal that connects them to the universal spirit. In moments of heart-centered presence, the seeker feels this divine connection most acutely, experiencing a profound sense of oneness with all that is.

In their journey, the seeker encounters the challenges of staying heart-centered in a world that often values logic over love. They learn to navigate these challenges with grace, staying true to their heart's path even when it diverges from the mainstream. This commitment to heart-centered living becomes a testament to their courage and authenticity.

Finally, the seeker realizes that heart-centered living is a lifelong practice, a continual return to love, compassion, and intuition as guiding principles. By dedicating themselves to this path, the seeker not only transforms their own life but also contributes to a more loving and connected world, one heart at a time.

In "The Wisdom of Solitude," the seeker embarks on a profound exploration of the enriching silence and sacred space that solitude offers. This journey is an inward voyage to the depths of the self, where the seeker discovers the transformative power of solitude. They learn that solitude is not loneliness but a fertile ground for growth, self-discovery, and deep spiritual connection.

The journey begins with the seeker recognizing the value of intentional solitude. They see it as an opportunity to disconnect from the external noise and distractions of the world, to connect more deeply with their inner voice. This deliberate embrace of solitude becomes a practice of self-care and spiritual nourishment.

In the quiet embrace of solitude, the seeker finds clarity and insight. Without the constant input and opinions of others, they are able to hear their own thoughts and feelings more clearly. This clarity brings about a deeper understanding of their desires, fears, and dreams, guiding their path with newfound wisdom.

Solitude teaches the seeker the art of self-reflection. In the stillness, they engage in introspective practices that reveal hidden aspects of their being. This self-reflection is a gateway to personal transformation, as the seeker confronts, accepts, and integrates the various facets of their identity.

The seeker discovers that solitude is a space for creativity and imagination to flourish. Freed from external constraints and influences, they tap into a wellspring of inspiration that lies within. This creative freedom leads to authentic expressions of the self, whether in art, writing, or other forms of creation.

In the practice of solitude, the seeker cultivates a deeper spiritual connection. They find that in the silence, they are more attuned to the subtle whispers of the divine. This spiritual communion brings a sense of peace and oneness, grounding the seeker in a profound sense of belonging to something greater.

Solitude becomes a teacher of resilience and independence for the seeker. They learn to enjoy their own company and find contentment within themselves. This self-sufficiency is empowering, reducing the dependence on external validation and companionship.

The seeker realizes that solitude offers a unique perspective on the interconnectedness of all life. In the quiet of being alone, they sense the invisible threads that connect them to the universe. This realization fosters a sense of unity and compassion that extends beyond their solitary experience.

Solitude challenges the seeker to confront their fears of being alone. Through this confrontation, they uncover a newfound strength and courage. Embracing solitude helps dissolve these fears, revealing that solitude can be a source of joy and fulfillment.

The wisdom of solitude teaches the seeker about the balance between solitude and community. They understand that both are essential to the human experience. Solitude enriches their interactions with others, as they bring a more centered, present, and authentic self to their relationships.

Finally, the seeker recognizes that the wisdom of solitude is an ongoing discovery. Each period of solitude offers new insights, growth, and deepening of the self. By honoring these sacred times of solitude, the seeker continually evolves, weaving the insights gained in solitude into the fabric of their daily life.

In "The Healing Power of Nature," the seeker embarks on a journey to reconnect with the Earth's wisdom and restorative energies. This exploration is an immersion into the natural world, where the seeker experiences the profound healing and grounding effects of being in harmony with nature. They discover that nature is not just a backdrop for life but an active, nurturing presence that offers solace, inspiration, and profound healing.

The journey begins with the seeker recognizing nature as a sanctuary, a place of refuge from the hustle and bustle of modern life. They find solace in the rhythms of nature—the cycle of seasons, the rise and fall of tides, the dance of the stars. This reconnection with nature's rhythms brings a sense of peace and grounding to the seeker's spirit.

In the embrace of nature, the seeker finds a profound sense of healing. Whether it's the soothing sound of a babbling brook, the majestic sight of a mountain range, or the gentle caress of a breeze, nature's elements work in subtle ways to heal the body, calm the mind, and rejuvenate the soul.

The seeker learns to observe nature's resilience and adaptability, drawing inspiration from the way nature endures and thrives despite challenges. This observation becomes a metaphor for the seeker's own life, teaching them resilience in the face of adversity and the ability to bloom where they are planted.

Nature teaches the seeker the art of mindfulness and presence. Immersed in the natural world, they become acutely aware of the beauty and intricacy of life. This mindful presence in nature leads to a deeper appreciation for the miracle of existence and the interconnectedness of all living things.

The seeker discovers that nature is a rich source of creativity and imagination. The natural world, with its endless forms, colors, and patterns, sparks the seeker's creativity, inspiring new ideas and artistic expressions. The limitless diversity of nature encourages the seeker to think outside the box and explore new avenues of creativity.

In their communion with nature, the seeker learns the lessons of impermanence and change. Observing the natural cycles of growth, decay, and renewal, they come to understand and accept the transient nature of life. This acceptance brings a sense of peace and helps the seeker to let go of clinging to the impermanent.

Nature becomes a teacher of simplicity and contentment for the seeker. Surrounded by the simplicity of the natural world, they are reminded of the beauty and sufficiency of the essentials. This realization encourages a shift towards a simpler, more sustainable way of living that honors the Earth and its resources.

The seeker finds that time spent in nature enhances their physical well-being. The fresh air, natural light, and physical activity inherent in exploring the outdoors contribute to improved health and vitality. This physical connection to the Earth strengthens the seeker's overall well-being, aligning body, mind, and spirit.

Through the healing power of nature, the seeker develops a deep sense of gratitude and stewardship for the Earth. Recognizing the gifts that nature bestows, they feel compelled to protect and preserve the natural world. This sense of responsibility deepens their connection to the Earth, turning them into an advocate for environmental conservation and sustainability.

Finally, the seeker understands that the healing power of nature is an endless wellspring of rejuvenation and inspiration. They commit to regularly immersing themselves in nature, knowing that each encounter with the natural world brings deeper healing, greater wisdom, and an enhanced sense of unity with all of creation. By weaving the healing power of nature into the fabric of their life, the seeker not only nurtures their own spirit but also contributes to the healing of the planet.

In "The Alchemy of Joyful Living," the seeker embarks on a luminous journey to cultivate a life brimming with joy and delight. This exploration delves into the transformative practices that convert everyday experiences into sources of joy, uncovering the alchemy that turns ordinary moments into extraordinary treasures. The seeker learns that joy is not a fleeting emotion but a profound state of being that arises from deep within, radiating outward to illuminate every aspect of life.

The journey begins with the seeker recognizing joy as an inherent aspect of their being, not contingent on external circumstances. They learn to tap into this inner wellspring of joy, finding that it is always accessible, even in the midst of challenge or adversity. This realization empowers the seeker to cultivate joy as a constant companion on their journey.

In the alchemy of joyful living, the seeker discovers the power of gratitude as a catalyst for joy. By focusing on the blessings and gifts in their life, they amplify the feeling of joy, transforming their perspective to one of abundance and wonder. This practice of gratitude becomes a daily ritual that continually opens their heart to joy.

The seeker finds that joy is often found in the simplest of moments. They learn to slow down and savor the beauty of the present, finding delight in the warmth of the sun, the laughter of a friend, or the tranquility of a quiet moment. This mindful appreciation of the ordinary brings a sense of enchantment and joy to everyday life.

Joyful living involves embracing playfulness and curiosity. The seeker rediscovers the childlike wonder that marvels at the world's mysteries and delights in exploration and play. This playful spirit infuses their life with lightness, creativity, and a sense of adventure.

The seeker learns that joy is magnified when shared with others. They seek to create and participate in experiences that bring joy to those around them, finding that their own joy is deepened in the process. This shared joy fosters connection, unity, and a collective upliftment that enhances the seeker's sense of belonging and community.

In cultivating joyful living, the seeker embraces the full spectrum of human emotions, understanding that joy does not exclude other feelings. They learn that acknowledging and experiencing all emotions authentically is integral to a joyful life, as it leads to greater depth, resilience, and capacity for joy.

The seeker discovers that acts of kindness and generosity are powerful alchemists of joy. By extending love and support to others, they experience a profound sense of joy that comes from giving. This altruistic joy reinforces the seeker's commitment to living a heart-centered life that contributes positively to the world.

Joyful living also involves aligning with one's passions and purpose. The seeker explores activities and pursuits that light up their soul, finding that engagement with their passions brings a deep, fulfilling joy. This alignment with their true self ensures that their life is an authentic expression of joy.

Finally, the seeker understands that the alchemy of joyful living is a continuous journey of discovery and practice. They commit to nurturing joy in themselves and others, knowing that each moment of joy is a precious stone in the mosaic of their life. By embracing the alchemy of joyful living, the seeker transforms their existence into a radiant expression of happiness and contentment. They realize that joy is not a destination but a manner of traveling, coloring each day with a spectrum of positivity and light.

The seeker acknowledges that challenges and sorrows are part of the human experience, but they learn to approach these with a resilient spirit, finding ways to reclaim joy even in difficult times. This resilience ensures that joy becomes an indestructible essence within, a beacon that guides them through life's ups and downs.

Through the alchemy of joyful living, the seeker becomes an embodiment of joy, inspiring others to discover and nurture their joy. Their life becomes a testament to the transformative power of living with an open heart, showing that joy is not only possible but essential for a fulfilling life.

The seeker finds that the pursuit of joy is also a spiritual practice, connecting them to the divine essence that permeates all of existence. In moments of true joy, they touch the infinite, experiencing a transcendence that lifts them beyond the mundane and into the realm of the sacred.

Joyful living teaches the seeker about the impermanence of life and the importance of cherishing each moment. They learn to live fully in the now, embracing life's fleeting nature with a spirit of gratitude and joy. This awareness deepens their appreciation for the preciousness of each experience, each connection, and each breath.

The alchemy of joyful living becomes a creative force in the seeker's life, inspiring them to craft a life that reflects their deepest desires and highest aspirations. They see life as a canvas for their joy, painting it with the vibrant colors of love, laughter, and light.

In their heart, the seeker carries the wisdom that joy is not dependent on external conditions but is a choice and an attitude towards life. They cultivate an inner environment where joy can thrive, regardless of external circumstances, making joy a constant, unwavering presence in their life.

The journey of joyful living reveals to the seeker that joy is a form of resistance against despair and negativity. By choosing joy, they affirm the goodness and beauty of life, countering the forces of darkness with the irrepressible light of their spirit.

As the seeker continues on the path of joyful living, they understand that this journey is infinite, with endless layers and dimensions of joy to explore. They remain open to the evolving nature of joy, welcoming new expressions and experiences of this sublime state of being.

Ultimately, the seeker's journey through the alchemy of joyful living becomes a profound spiritual journey, one that leads them to the heart of their being and the essence of the universe. In this sacred space, they find that joy is the natural state of the soul, a divine gift that illuminates the path back to the source.

In "The Dance of Intimacy and Independence," the seeker explores the delicate balance between deepening connections with others and nurturing their own sovereign spirit. This journey is an artful exploration of how to engage in meaningful relationships while maintaining a sense of self and personal freedom. The seeker discovers that true intimacy does not confine but expands the heart, allowing for a harmonious blend of togetherness and individuality.

The journey begins with the understanding that intimacy is a profound connection that transcends physical proximity, touching the very essence of beings. The seeker learns that to cultivate such connections, they must first be intimate with themselves, understanding and embracing their depths, desires, and boundaries.

In navigating the dance of intimacy and independence, the seeker finds that communication is key. They learn to express their needs, desires, and boundaries with clarity and compassion, fostering an environment of trust and mutual respect in their relationships. This open dialogue becomes the foundation for a healthy balance between closeness and personal space.

The seeker discovers the importance of self-love in the dance of intimacy and independence. They realize that by loving and valuing themselves, they bring a whole and fulfilled self to their relationships. This self-love prevents dependency, allowing intimacy to flourish without compromising independence.

In their exploration, the seeker encounters the challenge of vulnerability. They learn that allowing themselves to be seen, with all their imperfections and fears, is essential for deep intimacy. Yet, this vulnerability is balanced with a strong sense of self, knowing that their worth is not diminished by their flaws or the perceptions of others.

The seeker finds that time alone is not in opposition to intimacy but is a vital component of it. They cherish moments of solitude as opportunities for self-reflection and growth. This personal time enriches their relationships, as they return to their connections refreshed and with new insights to share.

The dance of intimacy and independence teaches the seeker about the fluidity of roles and relationships. They understand that each relationship is unique and that the balance between closeness and autonomy shifts and changes. This flexibility allows the seeker to navigate relationships with grace, honoring the needs of the moment.

The seeker learns that independence in relationships is not about physical distance but emotional and spiritual freedom. They cultivate relationships where each person is encouraged to pursue their passions, dreams, and spiritual journey, knowing that this individual growth enhances their shared experience.

In their journey, the seeker discovers that the dance of intimacy and independence is one of constant learning and adjustment. They remain open to the lessons each relationship brings, willing to adapt and grow. This openness ensures that their relationships are alive, dynamic, and evolving.

Finally, the seeker realizes that the balance between intimacy and independence is an ongoing dance, a beautiful interplay of connection and freedom. By embracing this dance, the seeker experiences the richness of deep connections without losing themselves, celebrating the joy of togetherness and the sanctity of their individual journey.

In "The Harmony of Giving and Receiving," the seeker delves into the dynamic equilibrium of generosity and receptivity that enriches life's exchanges. This exploration uncovers the beauty of a balanced flow between giving of oneself and openly receiving the gifts of the universe. The seeker learns that this harmony is essential for personal growth, meaningful relationships, and the circulation of abundance and love in the world.

The journey begins with the realization that giving and receiving are two sides of the same coin, interconnected and equally important.

The seeker understands that an imbalance—whether it's giving without receiving or receiving without giving—leads to disharmony and depletion. This awareness becomes the foundation for cultivating a balanced life.

In mastering the harmony of giving and receiving, the seeker discovers the joy of selfless giving. They learn that giving from the heart, without expectation of return, brings a profound sense of fulfillment and connection. This selfless generosity becomes a source of inner joy and abundance, reflecting the seeker's deep well of love and compassion.

The seeker learns the importance of receiving with grace and gratitude. They understand that receiving is not merely taking but an act of allowing oneself to be nourished and supported. By accepting gifts, help, and love openly, the seeker honors the giver and completes the cycle of generosity, fostering a culture of mutual appreciation and support.

The seeker finds that the harmony of giving and receiving is deeply intertwined with self-worth. They realize that feeling deserving of love, support, and abundance is crucial for healthy receptivity. This sense of worthiness empowers the seeker to receive joyfully, knowing that they are as worthy of receiving as they are capable of giving.

In navigating the balance of giving and receiving, the seeker encounters the challenge of boundaries. They learn to give generously while also respecting their limits, ensuring that their giving comes from a place of abundance rather than obligation or depletion. This boundary-setting ensures that their generosity remains sustainable and joy-filled.

The harmony of giving and receiving

teaches the seeker about the flow of energy in relationships and the universe. They come to understand that just as nature operates in cycles of giving and receiving, so do human interactions. By aligning with this natural flow, the seeker enhances the health and vitality of their relationships, ensuring a reciprocal exchange of support and kindness.

The seeker discovers that gratitude plays a pivotal role in the harmony of giving and receiving. By cultivating a grateful heart, both when giving and receiving, they amplify the positive energy of the exchange. Gratitude transforms even the simplest acts of giving and receiving into meaningful, soul-enriching experiences.

In their journey, the seeker learns to release any guilt associated with receiving. They recognize that receiving with joy and appreciation is as much a gift to the giver as the gift itself. This release of guilt opens the seeker to a more abundant flow of love, resources, and opportunities.

The seeker finds that the harmony of giving and receiving is not just about material gifts but also about the exchange of time, energy, knowledge, and emotional support. They become more mindful of the many ways they give to and receive from others, valuing all forms of exchange as essential to the tapestry of human connection.

Through the practice of balanced giving and receiving, the seeker becomes a conduit for abundance. They see themselves as part of a larger ecosystem of generosity, where each act of giving and open-hearted receiving strengthens the bonds of community and spreads ripples of kindness and love.

The seeker realizes that maintaining the harmony of giving and receiving requires constant attention and intention. They commit to staying attuned to the needs of the moment, whether it calls for giving, receiving, or a delicate balance of both. This commitment ensures that their life remains a dynamic dance of generosity and gratitude.

Finally, the seeker understands that the harmony of giving and receiving is a fundamental principle of the universe, mirroring the balance found in nature. By embodying this principle, the seeker not only enriches their own life but also contributes to the greater flow of love and abundance in the world, participating in the sacred cycle of giving and receiving that sustains all life.

In "Cultivating Spiritual Patience," the seeker embarks on a journey to embrace the unfolding of life with grace and trust. This exploration delves into the virtue of patience as a cornerstone of spiritual growth, revealing how it can transform challenges into opportunities for deepening faith and understanding. The seeker discovers that spiritual patience is not passive waiting but an active engagement with life, marked by a calm and trusting acceptance of divine timing.

The journey begins with the seeker recognizing the pace of life often doesn't align with personal timelines. They learn to release the grip of urgency and immediacy, understanding that some of the most profound developments require time to blossom. This shift in perspective brings a sense of peace, even in the midst of delays and uncertainties.

In cultivating spiritual patience, the seeker finds solace in the natural world, observing how each season unfolds in its own time, each flower blooms at the perfect moment. These observations reinforce the seeker's trust in the natural rhythm of life, encouraging them to mirror this trust in their personal journey.

The seeker discovers that spiritual patience is deeply intertwined with faith. They learn to trust in a higher plan, believing that everything happens for a reason, even if that reason isn't immediately apparent. This trust fosters a patient heart, one that can wait with hope and expectation for the mysteries of life to unfold.

In their practice of spiritual patience, the seeker learns the art of presence. They find that by being fully in the moment, the impatience for the future diminishes. This presence allows them to savor the journey, finding joy and lessons in the here and now, rather than constantly looking ahead.

The seeker realizes that spiritual patience is a form of surrender. They learn to let go of the need to control outcomes, trusting that the universe will deliver what is needed at the perfect time. This surrender is not a sign of weakness but a powerful statement of faith and strength.

Spiritual patience teaches the seeker about resilience and perseverance. They understand that patience is not merely waiting but continuing to move forward with a steady heart, even when progress seems slow or invisible. This perseverance in the face of adversity becomes a testament to the seeker's spiritual maturity and depth.

The seeker finds that spiritual patience enhances their relationships. By practicing patience with others, they cultivate understanding, empathy, and deeper connections. This patience becomes a gift not only to themselves but to those around them, fostering a more compassionate and supportive community.

In the quiet moments of reflection, the seeker contemplates the transformative power of spiritual patience. They see how it has shaped their character, deepened their faith, and enriched their life's journey. This contemplation fills the seeker with gratitude for the lessons and growth that patience has brought into their life.

Finally, the seeker understands that cultivating spiritual patience is a lifelong endeavor. It is a virtue that grows and deepens with each challenge, each

waiting period, and each moment of uncertainty. By committing to the practice of spiritual patience, the seeker not only navigates the ebb and flow of life with grace but also becomes a beacon of calm and trust in a world that often rushes and hurries. This embodiment of patience inspires others to embrace the journey with a more tranquil heart, spreading a wave of serenity and acceptance that transcends the immediate demands of the external world.

The seeker learns that spiritual patience is an expression of love—love for the self, for others, and for the divine journey of life. It is an acknowledgment that growth, healing, and understanding cannot be rushed, that they unfold in the fullness of time, wrapped in the wisdom of the universe. This love-infused patience becomes a nurturing force, encouraging the seeker and those around them to bloom in their own time, without force or haste.

Through the cultivation of spiritual patience, the seeker discovers a profound sense of alignment with the universe. They come to see that their personal rhythm, when attuned to the cosmic flow, creates a harmonious dance with life's unfolding. This alignment brings a sense of belonging and purpose, grounding the seeker in the comforting embrace of divine timing.

The practice of spiritual patience brings unexpected gifts and insights. The seeker finds that in the spaces of waiting and stillness, new dimensions of their being are revealed. These quiet moments become opportunities for deep introspection and revelation, uncovering hidden strengths and visions for the future.

The seeker comes to cherish the moments of pause and delay as sacred pauses in the symphony of life. They recognize these intervals as essential breaths, allowing space for reflection, gratitude, and preparation for the next movement. This appreciation transforms waiting from a challenge to a cherished part of the journey, imbued with potential and grace.

In their heart, the seeker carries the wisdom that spiritual patience is a key to inner peace. They understand that by embracing life's timing with a patient heart, they flow with life rather than resist it, finding peace even in uncertainty. This inner peace becomes a steady light, guiding them through life's inevitable twists and turns.

As the seeker continues on their path, they realize that spiritual patience is not a destination but a way of walking the journey. It is a companion that whispers words of encouragement, reminding them to trust, to wait, and to love the journey in all its phases. By walking with patience, the seeker's path is marked by a deeper sense of fulfillment and a profound connection to the rhythm of the cosmos.

Ultimately, the seeker's journey through the cultivation of spiritual patience becomes a profound spiritual practice in itself, a testament to the beauty of life's unfolding mystery. It is a practice that enriches the tapestry of their existence, weaving threads of tranquility, trust, and timeless wisdom into the fabric of their days.

In "The Illumination of Inner Wisdom," the seeker embarks on a profound journey to uncover the deep, intuitive knowledge that resides within their soul. This exploration delves into the realms of self-awareness and introspection, where the seeker discovers that true wisdom is not acquired but revealed. The seeker learns that inner wisdom is a guiding light, offering clarity, insight, and direction on the spiritual path.

The journey begins with the understanding that inner wisdom is an inherent aspect of the seeker's being, a sacred compass embedded in their essence. The seeker learns to quiet the external noise and internal chatter to connect with this inner guidance. This connection to their core illuminates the path forward, offering solace and certainty in moments of doubt and confusion.

In cultivating a relationship with their inner wisdom, the seeker finds that solitude and silence are invaluable allies. They create sacred spaces for stillness and reflection, allowing the voice of their inner wisdom to emerge. These moments of quiet communion become a wellspring of insight, enriching the seeker's journey with profound understanding and enlightenment.

The seeker discovers that inner wisdom often speaks through the language of intuition and feelings. They learn to trust these subtle nudges and emotional currents, recognizing them as messages from the depths of their being. This trust in their intuitive guidance fosters a deeper sense of alignment with their true path and purpose.

Inner wisdom teaches the seeker about the power of discernment. They come to understand that not all thoughts, opinions, and advice align with their highest good. The seeker cultivates the ability to discern which voices to heed and which to release, guided by the unwavering clarity of their inner wisdom.

The seeker finds that inner wisdom is closely linked to authenticity. By living in accordance with their inner truths, they honor their wisdom and reinforce their connection to it. This authenticity becomes a beacon, attracting experiences, relationships, and opportunities that resonate with the seeker's true self.

In their quest for inner wisdom, the seeker learns the value of reflection and self-inquiry. They engage in practices such as journaling, meditation, and contemplation, delving into the depths of their psyche. These practices illuminate the hidden corners of their being, bringing to light the wisdom that lies within.

The seeker realizes that inner wisdom is not static but dynamic, evolving with their spiritual journey. They remain open to new insights and revelations, understanding that wisdom grows with experience. This openness ensures that the seeker's inner wisdom remains a vibrant and relevant guide, reflecting their continual growth and understanding.

Inner wisdom fosters a profound sense of peace and trust in the seeker. Armed with the knowledge that they carry a wellspring of wisdom within, they navigate life's challenges with a calm assurance. This inner peace is a testament to the strength and reliability of their inner wisdom, offering stability amidst life's uncertainties.

The seeker learns that sharing their inner wisdom is a gift to the world. By expressing their insights and revelations, they contribute to the collective pool of knowledge and understanding. This sharing of wisdom is an act of service, lighting the way for others on their spiritual journeys.

Finally, the seeker understands that the illumination of inner wisdom is an ongoing process, a journey that deepens with each step. By continually seeking to connect with and express their inner wisdom, the seeker not only enriches their own life but also serves as a guiding light for others. This dedication to inner wisdom transforms the seeker's journey into a beacon of clarity, insight, and inspiration, illuminating the path for all who seek to find their way.

Chapter 7

In "The Symphony of Cosmic Unity," the seeker ventures into the vast expanse of the cosmos, exploring the intricate harmony that binds all of existence. This journey is a profound realization of the interconnectedness that weaves through the fabric of the universe, a tapestry where every thread is essential, and every pattern holds meaning. The seeker discovers that this cosmic symphony is not just an external phenomenon but resonates within the core of their being, linking them to the grand orchestration of life.

The journey begins with the awe-inspiring recognition that the universe operates in a state of perfect harmony, where galaxies, stars, and planets move in an elegant dance governed by cosmic laws. The seeker sees this celestial ballet as a reflection of the same harmony that governs the microscopic world of atoms and molecules, realizing that the macrocosm and microcosm are mirror images, bound by the same unifying principles.

In tuning into the symphony of cosmic unity, the seeker learns to listen with the heart, sensing the subtle vibrations that connect all forms of life. This attunement to the universal heartbeat fosters a profound sense of belonging and kinship with the cosmos, dissolving feelings of separation and isolation.

The seeker discovers that cosmic unity is echoed in the natural world, where ecosystems demonstrate intricate interdependence and balance. This realization deepens the seeker's respect for the Earth and all its inhabitants, inspiring a commitment to live in harmony with nature, honoring the delicate web of life that sustains us all.

In their exploration, the seeker finds that cosmic unity transcends physical boundaries, extending into the realms of energy and spirit. They understand that thoughts, emotions, and intentions contribute to the collective energy field, influencing the tapestry of existence. This awareness motivates the seeker to cultivate positive, loving energies, contributing to the overall harmony of the cosmos.

The seeker learns that cosmic unity is the foundation of genuine compassion and empathy. Recognizing the interconnectedness of all beings fosters a deep sense of solidarity and understanding, driving the seeker to act with kindness and consideration, knowing that each action reverberates through the cosmic web.

In the silent moments of meditation and contemplation, the seeker experiences moments of profound unity, where the illusion of separation melts away, revealing the underlying oneness of all existence. These mystical experiences become touchstones of truth, guiding the seeker's journey and deepening their commitment to living as a conscious part of the cosmic symphony.

The seeker realizes that the symphony of cosmic unity is an invitation to participate actively in the dance of existence. They see their life as a unique melody within the greater composition, understanding that their thoughts, words, and actions contribute to the harmony or discord of the whole. This realization inspires the seeker to live with intention and purpose, aligning their personal rhythm with the universal harmony.

In their journey, the seeker encounters challenges and discord, both within and without. They learn that dissonance is part of the cosmic symphony, providing contrast and opportunities for growth. Embracing these challenges with grace and trust, the seeker finds ways to restore harmony, guided by the wisdom of cosmic unity.

Finally, the seeker understands that the symphony of cosmic unity is an eternal song, an ever-evolving melody that encompasses all of time and space. By embracing their place in this grand orchestration, the seeker lives with a sense of wonder, joy, and reverence for the sacred dance of existence, contributing their unique voice to the chorus of the cosmos.

In "The Alchemy of Spiritual Transformation," the seeker embarks on an inner odyssey, delving into the transformative processes that lead to profound personal and spiritual growth. This journey is marked by a series of metamorphoses, where the seeker undergoes deep changes that refine their essence and elevate their consciousness. The seeker discovers that spiritual transformation is akin to alchemy, where the base elements of the self are transmuted into spiritual gold, revealing the luminous core of their being.

The journey begins with the seeker's willingness to enter the crucible of transformation, embracing the fires of challenge, change, and self-exploration. They understand that true transformation requires courage to face the unknown, to let go of the familiar, and to confront the shadows within. This courage is the first step in the alchemical process, igniting the flame of change.

In the heat of transformation, the seeker encounters their inner demons and unhealed wounds. They learn that these challenges are not obstacles but essential components of the alchemical process. By facing and integrating these aspects of themselves, the seeker initiates a powerful process of purification, shedding layers of illusion and falsehood.

The seeker discovers the importance of dissolution, where old identities, beliefs, and attachments are broken down. This stage of the alchemical journey is marked by uncertainty and vulnerability but is essential for new growth. The seeker learns to trust in the process, surrendering to the dissolution as a necessary step towards rebirth. In this space of letting go, they find the freedom to imagine new possibilities for their life, unencumbered by past limitations.

As the seeker moves through the stages of alchemy, they encounter the phase of coagulation, where the insights and lessons gleaned from their journey begin to solidify into a new sense of self. This emerging self is more aligned with their true essence, forged in the fires of transformation and imbued with a deeper wisdom and authenticity.

The seeker learns that spiritual transformation is not a solitary journey but one that is enriched by the guidance of mentors, the wisdom of ancient traditions, and the support of a like-minded community. These external influences act as catalysts in the alchemical process, offering new perspectives and encouraging the seeker to delve deeper into their inner work.

In their quest for transformation, the seeker embraces the practice of inner alchemy, engaging in meditation, contemplation, and other spiritual disciplines that facilitate self-transcendence. These practices become sacred rituals that support the seeker's metamorphosis, helping them to connect with the divine spark within.

The seeker finds that spiritual transformation is a cyclical process, with each cycle bringing them closer to their highest potential. They come to embrace the perpetual nature of growth, understanding that each phase of transformation prepares them for the next, in an ever-upward spiral of evolution.

The alchemy of spiritual transformation teaches the seeker about the interplay of light and shadow, revealing that true growth encompasses both. They learn to integrate their light and dark aspects, recognizing that wholeness comes from embracing the full spectrum of their being. This integration is a key alchemical achievement, bringing balance and harmony to the seeker's spirit.

Through the process of spiritual transformation, the seeker cultivates a profound inner peace and a resilient joy that is not shaken by external circumstances. They discover an unshakeable core within, a sanctuary of calm and strength that supports them through life's trials and triumphs.

Finally, the seeker understands that the alchemy of spiritual transformation is an ongoing journey of becoming. With each step, they shed the old to reveal the new, continuously expanding their consciousness and embodying a greater expression of their divine essence. By committing to this path of alchemical change, the seeker becomes a living testament to the power of transformation, inspiring others to embark on their own journeys of spiritual alchemy.

In "The Tapestry of Spiritual Traditions," the seeker explores the rich mosaic of spiritual paths that humanity has woven throughout history. This journey is an expansive exploration of the diverse ways in which cultures around the world have sought to understand the sacred and the divine. The seeker discovers that each tradition is a unique thread in the larger tapestry of spiritual wisdom, offering valuable insights and practices that enrich the seeker's own spiritual journey.

The journey begins with the seeker's curiosity and respect for the variety of spiritual expressions that exist. They delve into the teachings, rituals, and sacred texts of various traditions, finding common themes of love, compassion, connection, and the quest for enlightenment. This exploration reveals the universality of the spiritual quest, transcending cultural and historical boundaries.

In their exploration, the seeker encounters the mystical branches of major world religions, discovering the esoteric teachings that lie at the heart of many faiths. They find that mysticism offers a direct, experiential approach to the divine, emphasizing personal revelation and the inner transformation of the seeker.

The seeker learns that each spiritual tradition offers unique practices and paths to transcendence. Whether through meditation, prayer, ritual, or service, these practices are tools that help the seeker connect with the divine and cultivate their inner life. The seeker adopts and adapts these practices, weaving them into their own spiritual tapestry.

In navigating the tapestry of spiritual traditions, the seeker encounters the concept of syncretism, where elements from different paths blend to create new, hybrid forms of spirituality. They see this blending as a reflection of the evolving nature of spiritual expression, adapting to meet the needs and understanding of each generation.

The seeker discovers that engaging with diverse spiritual traditions fosters a deep sense of empathy and respect for the beliefs of others. This openness enriches their own spiritual journey, breaking down barriers of dogma and exclusivity, and promoting a more inclusive and compassionate worldview.

Through their exploration, the seeker finds that certain symbols, myths, and archetypes recur across many traditions, pointing to a collective spiritual heritage. These universal motifs offer profound insights into the human psyche and the nature of the divine, revealing the interconnectedness of all spiritual quests.

The seeker realizes that the tapestry of spiritual traditions is not just a historical or cultural artifact but a living, breathing entity. It continues to evolve as humanity's understanding of the divine deepens and expands. The seeker sees themselves as part of this ongoing evolution, contributing their own experiences and insights to the collective spiritual heritage.

In their journey through the tapestry of spiritual traditions, the seekerlearns the value of discernment and personal resonance. They understand that not every tradition or practice will align with their path, but each offers a potential gateway to deeper understanding. This discernment allows the seeker to navigate the vast landscape of spirituality with an open heart and a critical mind, embracing what resonates and respectfully setting aside what does not.

The seeker finds that engaging with various spiritual traditions not only broadens their understanding but also deepens their connection to their own spiritual roots. They come to appreciate the unique beauty and wisdom of their own tradition more fully, seeing it in the context of the global spiritual mosaic. This enriched perspective fosters a deeper commitment to their personal path, infused with a greater appreciation for the diversity of spiritual expression.

Through the tapestry of spiritual traditions, the seeker cultivates a global spiritual perspective, recognizing the interconnectedness of all paths that seek the truth. This realization brings a sense of unity and solidarity with seekers around the world, transcending differences and celebrating the shared journey toward enlightenment and understanding.

Finally, the seeker understands that the tapestry of spiritual traditions is a testament to humanity's perennial quest for meaning, purpose, and connection with the divine. By exploring and honoring this rich tapestry, the seeker not only enriches their own spiritual journey but also participates in the collective human endeavor to understand the sacred mysteries of existence. This participation is both a privilege and a responsibility, inspiring the seeker to live with greater awareness, compassion, and reverence for the sacred diversity of life's spiritual expressions.

In "Embracing Spiritual Diversity," the seeker delves into the rich spectrum of beliefs, practices, and experiences that constitute the spiritual landscape of humanity. This journey is an exploration of the myriad ways in which individuals and cultures express their understanding of, and relationship with, the divine. The seeker discovers that spiritual diversity is not a divide but a reflection of the infinite facets of the human spirit and the boundless nature of the sacred.

The journey begins with the seeker recognizing that each spiritual path, with its unique rituals, symbols, and doctrines, is a reflection of the human quest for meaning and connection. They learn to appreciate the beauty and depth of various traditions, seeing them as different paths leading to the same summit of spiritual realization.

In their exploration of spiritual diversity, the seeker encounters the concept of interfaith dialogue and the potential for mutual enrichment that it holds. They engage in conversations with individuals from diverse spiritual backgrounds, finding that these exchanges foster understanding, respect, and a shared sense of humanity's spiritual quest.

The seeker discovers that embracing spiritual diversity challenges and expands their own beliefs. They are encouraged to question, reflect, and grow, broadening their spiritual horizons. This process of exploration and inquiry deepens their own faith, making it more inclusive and compassionate.

Through their journey, the seeker learns that spiritual diversity is a mirror of the complexity and richness of the human experience. They come to understand that each tradition, with its unique insights and wisdom, contributes to the collective understanding of life's mysteries.

The seeker finds that embracing spiritual diversity cultivates empathy and compassion. By recognizing the sacredness in all paths, they open their heart to the struggles, joys, and aspirations of others, regardless of their spiritual orientation. This empathy becomes a bridge of understanding and solidarity among diverse spiritual communities.

In navigating the realm of spiritual diversity, the seeker becomes an advocate for spiritual pluralism, promoting an environment where different beliefs can coexist in harmony. They champion the idea that spiritual diversity is not a threat but an opportunity for growth, learning, and enrichment.

The seeker discovers that spiritual diversity is also reflected in personal spirituality, where individuals draw from various traditions to create a path that resonates with their unique experiences and understandings. This personalized approach to spirituality underscores the dynamic and evolving nature of the spiritual journey.

Through their engagement with spiritual diversity, the seeker experiences the unity underlying all spiritual expressions. They realize that at the core of every tradition lies the same longing for the divine, the same quest for transcendence and enlightenment. This realization fosters a deep sense of kinship with all seekers, transcending the boundaries of creed and dogma.

Finally, the seeker understands that embracing spiritual diversity is a continuous journey of learning, openness, and dialogue. By remaining curious and receptive to the vast array of spiritual expressions, the seeker not only enriches their own path but also contributes to a world where spiritual diversity is celebrated as a precious manifestation of the human spirit's quest for the sacred.

In "The Healing Journey of Forgiveness," the seeker embarks on a transformative path to release the burdens of resentment, anger, and hurt that obstruct the heart's peace. This journey is a deep dive into the essence of forgiveness, not as an act of condoning but as a profound process of liberation and healing. The seeker discovers that forgiveness is a key to unlocking inner peace, mending relationships, and reclaiming personal power.

The journey begins with the seeker acknowledging the pain and wounds inflicted by others or by their own actions. They confront the emotions and memories that have been held captive in the heart, recognizing that holding onto them serves only to perpetuate suffering.

In exploring the nature of forgiveness, the seeker learns that it is an act of strength and courage. They understand that to forgive requires a generous heart, willing to transcend the ego's desire for retribution and to see beyond the immediate hurt to the broader horizon of peace and reconciliation.

The seeker discovers that forgiveness is, first and foremost, a gift to oneself. By choosing to forgive, they release the toxic chains of bitterness and free themselves from the past's grip, allowing healing and renewal to flow into their life.

In their journey, the seeker encounters the wisdom of empathy and understanding. They learn to view the actions of others through a lens of compassion, considering the circumstances, pains, and fears that may have led to hurtful behaviors. This empathetic perspective facilitates the process of forgiveness, humanizing those who have caused pain.

The seeker finds that forgiveness is a process, not a single act. It may unfold over time, requiring patience, persistence, and self-compassion.

They embrace this process, allowing themselves to forgive in their own time and way, without forcing or rushing the healing.

Through the practice of forgiveness, the seeker experiences a deepening of their spiritual connection. They realize that forgiveness is a divine quality, reflecting the unconditional love and compassion at the heart of many spiritual traditions. By embodying forgiveness, the seeker aligns themselves with these higher principles, enhancing their spiritual growth and understanding.

The seeker learns that forgiveness also extends to self-forgiveness, which is often the most challenging form of forgiveness. They confront their own mistakes and shortcomings, offering themselves the same compassion and understanding they extend to others. This self-forgiveness is a crucial step towards inner peace and self-acceptance.

In navigating the healing journey of forgiveness, the seeker discovers the power of ritual and intention. They may engage in practices such as writing letters of forgiveness (sent or unsent), meditation focused on letting go, or symbolic acts of release. These rituals reinforce their commitment to forgiveness and facilitate the emotional and spiritual process of letting go.

The seeker finds that forgiveness opens the door to reconciliation and deeper connections. While forgiveness does not always mean re-establishing a relationship, it creates a space for new beginnings and healthier interactions, whether with others or within the seeker's own heart.

Through the practice of forgiveness, the seeker becomes a vessel of peace and healing, not only for themselves but for their community and the world at large. They understand that forgiveness is a potent force for transformation, capable of healing wounds, bridging divides, and fostering a culture of understanding and compassion.

Finally, the seeker recognizes that the healing journey of forgiveness is a lifelong path. As they continue to encounter challenges and conflicts, their capacity for forgiveness deepens, becoming a wellspring of resilience, peace, and profound spiritual wisdom. By embracing forgiveness as a way of life, the seeker contributes to their own well-being and to the creation of a more compassionate and forgiving world.

In "The Path to Inner Peace," the seeker embarks on a serene journey to cultivate a state of tranquility and harmony within their own being. This exploration delves into practices, mindsets, and lifestyle choices that foster a calm and centered spirit, despite the external world's turbulence. The seeker discovers that inner peace is not merely an absence of conflict but a profound presence of balance, contentment, and deep connection with the essence of life.

The journey begins with the seeker acknowledging the importance of mindfulness and presence in cultivating inner peace. They learn to anchor themselves in the present moment, letting go of anxieties about the future and regrets about the past. This practice of mindfulness brings a sense of calm and clarity, revealing the beauty and tranquility available in the now.

In their pursuit of inner peace, the seeker explores the art of meditation and contemplation. These practices become sanctuaries of silence and introspection, where the seeker can retreat from the noise of the external world and connect with their innermost self. Through regular meditation, the seeker cultivates a deep sense of stillness that permeates their daily life.

The seeker discovers the power of nature in nurturing inner peace. They find solace and rejuvenation in the natural world, whether walking through a forest, listening to the ocean's waves, or simply sitting under the sky. Nature's inherent tranquility resonates with the seeker's spirit, aligning them with the peaceful rhythms of the Earth.

In navigating the path to inner peace, the seeker learns the importance of simplicity and minimalism. By reducing clutter, commitments, and distractions, they create space in their life for what truly matters. This simplicity brings a sense of ease and spaciousness, allowing the seeker to move through life with a light and peaceful heart.

The seeker realizes that inner peace is closely linked to acceptance and letting go. They learn to accept life as it is, embracing its imperfections and uncertainties with grace. This acceptance frees the seeker from the turmoil of resistance and opens the door to a profound peace that accepts life's ebb and flow.

In their journey, the seeker encounters the value of compassion and kindness, both towards themselves and others. They understand that a compassionate heart is a peaceful heart. By practicing kindness and understanding, the seeker dissolves barriers of judgment and separation, fostering a sense of unity and peace within and around them.

The seeker finds that inner peace is nurtured through healthy relationships and connections. They cultivate relationships that are supportive, authentic, and nurturing, distancing themselves from dynamics that breed conflict and unrest. These harmonious connections become pillars of peace in the seeker's life, offering love and stability.

Through the path to inner peace, the seeker learns the importance of balance in all aspects of lifework, rest, activity, and solitude. They strive for a harmonious lifestyle that honors their needs and boundaries, ensuring that their energy is replenished, and their spirit remains serene.

Finally, the seeker understands that the path to inner peace is a continuous journey, woven into the fabric of daily life. They remain committed to practices that cultivate tranquility, approaching each day with an intention to live in peace. By embodying inner peace, the seeker becomes a beacon of calm in a chaotic world, inspiring others to find their own path to tranquility.

In "The Art of Conscious Living," the seeker embarks on an enlightened path that intertwines mindfulness, intentionality, and an acute awareness of life's interconnectedness. This journey is a deliberate choice to engage with the world in a more meaningful, present, and responsible manner, transforming everyday actions into acts of spiritual significance. The seeker discovers that conscious living is an art form, where each decision, interaction, and moment is infused with depth, purpose, and a profound respect for the web of life.

The journey begins with the seeker's commitment to mindfulness as the cornerstone of conscious living. They cultivate a practice of being fully present in each moment, experiencing life with all their senses, and engaging with the world with an open heart and mind. This mindfulness transforms mundane activities into rich, meaningful experiences, deepening the seeker's connection to the present.

In their pursuit of conscious living, the seeker explores the power of intention. They learn to set clear, positive intentions for their actions, interactions, and goals, infusing their life with direction and purpose. These intentions act as guiding lights, ensuring that the seeker's choices are aligned with their highest values and aspirations.

The seeker discovers the importance of ethical and sustainable living as expressions of consciousness. They make thoughtful choices about consumption, lifestyle, and environmental impact, striving to live in harmony with the Earth and its inhabitants. This ethical approach reflects the seeker's deep reverence for life and their commitment to contributing to a more conscious and sustainable world.

In navigating the art of conscious living, the seeker embraces the practice of gratitude. They cultivate an attitude of thankfulness for life's blessings, big
and small. This practice of gratitude opens the seeker's heart to the abundance that surrounds them, fostering a sense of contentment and joy that permeates their everyday life.

The seeker learns that conscious living involves deep listening—to themselves, to others, and to the world around them. They become attuned to the subtle messages and lessons that life offers, responding with empathy and understanding. This deep listening enhances their relationships and guides them in their journey, making each interaction more meaningful and connected.

In their journey, the seeker discovers the value of conscious communication. They choose their words with care, aiming to speak with honesty, kindness, and clarity. This mindful approach to communication fosters authentic connections and minimizes misunderstandings, contributing to a more harmonious and compassionate community.

The seeker finds that conscious living extends to their personal well-being. They attend to their physical, emotional, and spiritual health with intention and care, recognizing that a balanced and healthy self is essential for living consciously. This self-care is an act of respect for their own being and enables them to engage with the world from a place of strength and vitality.

Through the art of conscious living, the seeker explores the interconnectedness of all things. They see themselves as part of a larger whole, understanding that their choices and actions have ripples that extend far beyond their immediate environment. This awareness inspires the seeker to act with consideration and responsibility, honoring the delicate web of life.

The seeker learns that conscious living is a dynamic practice, evolving as they grow and learn. They remain open to new insights and perspectives, adapting their lifestyle and choices to reflect their deepening understanding of consciousness. This flexibility ensures that their path of conscious living is always fresh, relevant, and aligned with their spiritual journey.

Finally, the seeker understands that the art of conscious living is both a personal commitment and a collective journey. By choosing to live with awareness and intention, they not only transform their own life but also contribute to the collective awakening of humanity. The seeker's conscious choices inspire others to consider their own path, spreading the seeds of mindfulness, compassion, and sustainability in a world that yearns for deeper consciousness and connection.

In "Harmonizing Body, Mind, and Spirit," the seeker embarks on an integrative journey to align the physical, mental, and spiritual aspects of their being into a cohesive and harmonious whole. This exploration recognizes the interdependence of these facets and seeks to cultivate balance, health, and wholeness. The seeker discovers that true well-being arises from this holistic alignment, enabling a life of vitality, clarity, and spiritual depth.

The journey begins with the seeker understanding the importance of nurturing the body as the temple of the spirit. They adopt practices that honor the physical self, such as nutritious eating, regular exercise, and restorative rest, recognizing that physical well-being is foundational to mental and spiritual health.

In harmonizing the mind, the seeker delves into practices that cultivate mental clarity and emotional balance. They explore meditation, mindfulness, and reflective journaling as tools to calm the mind, manage stress, and foster a positive mental landscape. This mental harmony enhances the seeker's ability to connect with their inner wisdom and navigate life's challenges with equanimity.

The seeker learns that spiritual well-being is nurtured through connection, purpose, and transcendence. They engage in practices that deepen their spiritual connection, whether through prayer, nature, art, or service to others. This spiritual engagement brings a sense of meaning and interconnectedness, enriching the seeker's life with a sense of the sacred.

In their pursuit of holistic harmony, the seeker discovers the transformative power of breath. They practice conscious breathing techniques that bridge the body, mind, and spirit, using the breath as a tool to center themselves, regulate emotions, and access deeper states of consciousness.

The seeker finds that self-care is an essential component of harmonizing body, mind, and spirit. They prioritize self-care rituals that rejuvenate and nourish all levels of their being, understanding that self-love and compassion are key to holistic well-being.

Through their journey, the seeker explores the healing arts as pathways to integration. They may experiment with modalities such as yoga, tai chi, acupuncture, or energy healing, finding practices that resonate with their unique needs and support their journey toward balance and wholeness.

The seeker learns that harmonizing body, mind, and spirit involves listening attentively to their inner signals and needs. They cultivate an awareness that allows them to respond intuitively to their well-being, adjusting their practices and lifestyle in alignment with their evolving journey.

In navigating the path to holistic harmony, the seeker embraces the cycles and rhythms of life. They learn to flow with these natural cycles, honoring the ebb and flow of energy, motivation, and well-being. This alignment with life's rhythms fosters resilience and adaptability, supporting the seeker's journey through change and growth.

The seeker discovers that community and relationships play a vital role in harmonizing body, mind, and spirit. They seek connections that uplift and support their holistic well-being, engaging in communities that share their values and aspirations. These supportive relationships amplify the seeker's efforts to live in harmony and offer opportunities for shared growth and healing.

Finally, the seeker understands that harmonizing body, mind, and spirit is an ongoing journey of discovery and refinement. They remain committed to practices that foster integration and balance, viewing each day as an opportunity to nurture their whole being. By embracing this holistic approach, the seeker cultivates a life of profound well-being, inner peace, and spiritual depth, radiating harmony and balance from the inside out.

In "Cultivating Resilience and Adaptability," the seeker embarks on a journey to strengthen their inner fortitude and flexibility in the face of life's inevitable changes and challenges. This exploration delves into the qualities that enable one to navigate adversity with grace, learn from experience, and emerge stronger and wiser. The seeker discovers that resilience and adaptability are not inherent traits but skills that can be developed and honed, serving as invaluable allies on the spiritual path.

The journey begins with the seeker recognizing the value of resilience as the ability to withstand and recover from life's difficulties. They commit to fostering a resilient spirit, one that can endure setbacks without losing hope or vitality. This commitment involves embracing challenges as opportunities for growth and learning, transforming obstacles into stepping stones on the path of personal evolution.

In cultivating adaptability, the seeker learns the art of flexibility and openness to change. They understand that life is in constant flux and that rigidity hinders growth. By cultivating a flexible mindset, the seeker navigates transitions and uncertainties with ease, viewing change as a natural and enriching part of the human experience.

The seeker discovers that resilience is deeply connected to a sense of purpose and meaning. They find that having a clear sense of direction and a connection to something greater than themselves provides the strength to persevere through tough times. This sense of purpose acts as an anchor, keeping the seeker grounded and focused amidstthe storms of life.

In their pursuit of resilience, the seeker explores the power of positive thinking and optimism. They learn to reframe challenges, focusing on solutions and opportunities rather than dwelling on problems. This positive outlook fosters resilience, enabling the seeker to maintain hope and motivation even in the face of adversity.

The seeker finds that adaptability is enhanced by creativity and innovation. They embrace creative thinking as a tool for adapting to new situations, finding novel solutions to challenges, and exploring alternative paths. This creative approach keeps the seeker agile and responsive to the ever-changing landscape of life.

In cultivating resilience, the seeker recognizes the importance of emotional intelligence. They develop the ability to manage their emotions, practice empathy, and maintain emotional balance. This emotional resilience strengthens their capacity to cope with stress, navigate interpersonal dynamics, and remain centered in challenging times.

The seeker learns that resilience and adaptability are supported by a strong support network. They cultivate relationships with family, friends, and community members who provide encouragement, advice, and a listening ear. This supportive environment acts as a buffer against life's hardships, reminding the seeker that they are not alone in their journey.

Through their exploration, the seeker discovers that physical well-being is integral to resilience and adaptability. They prioritize self-care, healthy living, and regular physical activity, understanding that a healthy body supports a resilient and adaptable mind. This holistic approach to well-being empowers the seeker to face challenges with strength and vitality.

The seeker realizes that resilience and adaptability are forged in the crucible of experience. They embrace life's trials as opportunities for personal development, knowing that each challenge faced and overcome strengthens their resilience and hones their ability to adapt. This perspective transforms the seeker's relationship with adversity, viewing it as a valuable teacher rather than an enemy.

Finally, the seeker understands that cultivating resilience and adaptability is a lifelong process. They remain committed to personal growth, continuous learning, and self-reflection. By embracing resilience and adaptability as essential components of their spiritual journey, the seeker navigates life's ups and downs with grace and wisdom, ever evolving and expanding in response to the rich tapestry of human experience.

In "The Essence of Authentic Leadership," the seeker explores the transformative power of leading with integrity, purpose, and a deep connection to one's true self. This journey uncovers the principles of authentic leadership that inspire trust, foster collaboration, and empower others to realize their full potential. The seeker discovers that true leadership is not about authority or position but about embodying values that inspire and uplift those around them.

The journey begins with the seeker's introspection into their core values and beliefs. They understand that authentic leadership is rooted in self-awareness and a commitment to living in alignment with one's deepest truths. This alignment fosters genuine confidence and credibility, enabling the seeker to lead by example and inspire others with their integrity.

In embracing authentic leadership, the seeker cultivates empathy and compassion. They recognize the importance of understanding and caring for the needs, aspirations, and challenges of those they lead. This empathetic approach builds strong relationships and creates a supportive environment where everyone feels valued and understood.

The seeker learns that authentic leadership involves embracing vulnerability. By openly sharing their challenges, uncertainties, and growth journeys, they foster a culture of openness and trust. This vulnerability breaks down barriers, encouraging others to share their authentic selves and contribute fully to the collective vision.

In their pursuit of authentic leadership, the seeker emphasizes the power of purpose-driven action. They lead with a clear vision that transcends personal gain, focusing on the greater good and the positive impact they can create. This purpose-driven approach galvanizes collective effort and imbues the seeker's leadership with a sense of meaning and mission.

The seeker discovers that authentic leadership requires the courage to stand for one's convictions, even in the face of opposition or uncertainty. They develop the resilience to uphold their values and make difficult decisions guided by their principles. This steadfastness earns them respect and loyalty, reinforcing their role as a trusted leader.

Through their exploration, the seeker finds that authentic leadership is characterized by inclusivity and collaboration. They value diverse perspectives and foster a culture where everyone's voice is heard and respected. This inclusivity enriches decision-making and innovation, creating a sense of shared ownership and commitment to the collective goals.

The seeker realizes that authentic leadership involves continuous learning and personal growth. They remain open to feedback, embrace new ideas, and seek opportunities for development. This commitment to growth ensures that their leadership remains dynamic, responsive, and aligned with evolving challenges and opportunities.

In navigating the path of authentic leadership, the seeker cultivates mindfulness and presence. They lead with a calm and centered spirit, responding to challenges with clarity and equanimity. This presence inspires confidence and stability, guiding the seeker and their community through turbulent times with grace and wisdom.

Finally, the seeker understands that the essence of authentic leadership is to serve and uplift others. They see leadership as an opportunity to empower, mentor, and support the growth of those around them. By dedicating themselves to the well-being and success of others, the seeker embodies the highest ideals of leadership, leaving a lasting positive impact on their community and the world.

In "The Journey of Co-Creation with the Universe," the seeker embarks on an empowering path to actively participate in the unfolding of their destiny, in partnership with the cosmic forces. This exploration delves into the principles of manifestation, intention, and synchronicity, revealing how the seeker can align their personal will with the universal will to bring forth their deepest desires and contribute to the greater good. The seeker discovers that co-creation is an artful dance with the divine, a dynamic interplay of giving and receiving, acting and allowing.

The journey begins with the seeker's realization of their inherent creative power. They understand that they are not passive observers of their life but active participants with the ability to shape their reality. This recognition ignites a sense of responsibility and empowerment, motivating the seeker to engage consciously with the creative process.

In their pursuit of co-creation, the seeker cultivates a clear vision of their desires and intentions. They learn the importance of clarity and specificity in manifesting their goals, focusing their energy and attention on what they wish to bring into existence. This clarity acts as a beacon, guiding the seeker's actions and attracting the resources and opportunities needed to realize their vision.

The seeker discovers the significance of aligning their intentions with the highest good. They recognize that true co-creation is not about imposing their will but about harmonizing their desires with the universal flow and the well-being of all. This alignment ensures that their efforts contribute to the collective evolution and the balance of the cosmos.

In navigating the journey of co-creation, the seeker develops a deep trust in the timing and wisdom of the universe. They learn to surrender control and allow the universe to orchestrate the perfect circumstances and encounters. This trust in divine timing fosters patience and resilience, allowing the seeker to flow with life's natural rhythms.

The seeker finds that gratitude and appreciation are powerfulforces in the journey of co-creation. By cultivating a grateful heart, they amplify the positive energy around their intentions and attract more of what they appreciate into their life. This attitude of gratitude creates a vibrational match with abundance, opening the doors to receiving the universe's blessings.

In their exploration of co-creation, the seeker learns the importance of taking inspired action. While setting intentions and trusting the universe are crucial, the seeker understands that they must also take steps toward their goals. These actions, infused with inspiration and aligned with their vision, become powerful catalysts in the manifestation process.

The seeker discovers that obstacles and challenges encountered along the way are part of the co-creative process. They view these as opportunities for growth, refinement of their vision, and deepening of their trust in the universe. Each challenge is seen as a stepping stone, further aligning the seeker with their path of co-creation.

Through the journey of co-creation, the seeker becomes more attuned to signs, symbols, and synchronicities. They recognize these as messages from the universe, guiding and affirming their path. This awareness enhances the seeker's ability to navigate their journey with confidence, seeing the interconnectedness of all events and encounters.

The seeker realizes that co-creation is an ongoing dialogue with the universe. They maintain an open line of communication through meditation, prayer, and reflection, continually refining their desires and intentions based on their evolving understanding and insights. This dynamic conversation ensures that the seeker and the universe are in constant collaboration, co-authoring the story of their life.

Finally, the seeker understands that the journey of co-creation with the universe is a sacred partnership that extends beyond personal fulfillment. By aligning their creative endeavors with the universal will, the seeker contributes to the unfolding of the cosmic plan, serving the greater good. This realization imbues their journey with a sense of purpose and interconnectedness, affirming that their co-creative efforts are an integral part of the divine tapestry of existence.

Chapter 8

Enlightenment, often envisioned as the pinnacle of spiritual attainment, reveals itself in myriad forms, reflecting the rich tapestry of human experience and belief. This exploration delves into the diverse landscapes of enlightenment, illustrating that this sublime state transcends any definition, embodying a spectrum of realization and awakening across cultures and spiritual paths.

The explorer on this journey discovers that enlightenment in Eastern traditions, such as Buddhism and Hinduism, often emphasizes the dissolution of the individual ego and the realization of a universal self. This understanding contrasts yet complements the Western mystical perspective, which might focus more on the union with the divine and the illumination of the soul.

In the wanderer's heart, the quest for enlightenment awakens a profound appreciation for each individual's unique journey. They see that enlightenment is not a one-size-fits-all experience but a profoundly personal unfolding shaped by one's experiences, insights, and spiritual lineage.

The sojourner learns that enlightenment is often marked by profound insight and transformative realization, known as satori in Zen Buddhism or the night of the soul in Christian mysticism. These milestones, though varied, are universal signposts of spiritual awakening, guiding the pilgrim through their journey.

In contemplation of enlightenment's multifaceted nature, the voyager encounters the concept of non-dual awareness. In this state, distinctions between self and other, subject and object, dissolve into a seamless unity. This realization, central to Advaita Vedanta and certain strands of Buddhism, offers a powerful lens through which to view the interconnectedness of all existence.

The seeker finds that cultivating virtues such as compassion, serenity, and wisdom often accompanies the pursuit of enlightenment.

While serving as indicators of spiritual progress, these qualities also deepen the seeker's capacity to engage with the world from a place of enlightened presence.

Amidst their exploration, the traveler discovers that enlightenment can manifest in the ordinary moments of life, revealing the sacred in the mundane. This understanding, often highlighted in Taoism and Zen, emphasizes the presence of the divine in every breath and every step, inviting the seeker to awaken to the enlightenment inherent in each moment.

The Pathfinder understands that enlightenment is not merely an escape from the world but an engagement with it from a heightened state of consciousness. This perspective, echoed in engaged Buddhism and other activist spiritualities, challenges the seeker to apply their enlightened insights to serve the world.

In their journey, the navigator encounters teachings that suggest enlightenment is not the end but the beginning of a new phase of spiritual service and education. This role, embodied by the bodhisattva in Mahayana Buddhism, reflects the vow to attain enlightenment not just for oneself but for the benefit of all beings.

Finally, the traveler realizes that the multifaceted nature of enlightenment enriches the spiritual journey, offering a kaleidoscope of perspectives from which to draw wisdom. By embracing this diversity, the seeker weaves a rich tapestry of understanding, celebrating the many paths that lead to the summit of spiritual awakening.

In a spiritual awakening, the pilgrim discovers the essential interplay between stillness and action, a dynamic balance that fuels the journey toward enlightenment. This exploration reveals that spiritual progress requires both the inner work of contemplation and the outer expression of compassionate action, each aspect informing and enhancing the other.

The wayfarer learns that stillness, often cultivated through meditation, prayer, and reflection, is the foundation for deep spiritual insight. In these moments of calm, the seeker encounters the depths of their being, touching the infinite wellspring of wisdom that lies within. This inner sanctuary becomes a source of strength and clarity, guiding the seeker's steps on the path.

As the nomad delves deeper into the practice of stillness, they find that it is not an escape from the world but a preparation for engaged action. The insights gained in silence inform their interactions and decisions, imbuing their actions with intentionality and purpose.

In a spiritual awakening, the wayfarer uncovers the essential harmony between the inner sanctum of stillness and the vibrant dance of action. This delicate balance is revealed as a cornerstone of the quest for enlightenment, where moments of profound silence and dynamic engagement intertwine, each nourishing and informing the other on the path to awakening.

The pilgrim learns that stillness, cultivated through meditation, contemplation, and mindful observation, is the fertile ground for deep spiritual insights. Within the embrace of silence, the traveler taps into the wellspring of inner wisdom, uncovering truths that guide their journey and illuminate their understanding.

As the nomad delves into the practice of stillness, they find it is not an escape from the world but a foundational state that prepares them for purposeful action. The clarity and peace harvested in quiet moments become the beacon that lights their way, infusing their actions in the world with intention, compassion, and authenticity.

The voyager discovers that actual action in the spiritual context is not merely about outward doing but about aligned action that flows from a deep connection with the divine. This action is inspired, purposeful, and inherently imbued with the tranquility and insight garnered from moments of stillness.

In navigating the interplay of stillness and action, the seeker becomes adept at recognizing when to pause and turn inward and when to step forward and enact their inner visions in the world. This dynamic rhythm becomes a dance of intuition and discernment, guided by the heartbeat of spiritual awareness.

The traveler finds that action carries a transformative power when rooted in the fertile soil of stillness. Acts of kindness, service, and creation become expressions of the seeker's highest self, contributing to their growth and the upliftment of those around them.

The sojourner learns that the balance of stillness and action is mirrored in the natural world, where periods of growth and activity are balanced by rest and renewal. By aligning with these natural rhythms, the seeker harmonizes their spiritual journey with the ebb and flow of the cosmos.

In the crucible of stillness, the explorer confronts the shadows and challenges that arise on their path. In these quiet depths, the most profound healing and transformation occur, fortifying the seeker's spirit for the active part of their journey, where they bring their inner discoveries into the light of day.

The odyssey of balancing stillness and action teaches the wanderer that spiritual awakening is a dynamic process encompassing the full spectrum of human experience. By embracing the serenity of stillness and the vitality of action, the seeker weaves a rich tapestry of enlightenment marked by growth, service, and a profound connection to the divine.

Finally, the adept recognizes that the interplay of stillness and action is a lifelong journey, an ever-unfolding dance that evolves with each step on the path to enlightenment. This dance is a personal and collective journey where the seeker's harmonized actions contribute to the world's awakening, echoing the timeless dance of creation itself.

In the sacred journey towards enlightenment, the adept encounters the profound task of integrating the shadow and light within their being. This path unveils the necessity of acknowledging and embracing the darker facets of the self as essential counterparts to the light, illustrating that true wholeness arises from the union of these dual aspects.

The traveler learns that the shadow consists of those parts of themselves that have been repressed, ignored, or deemed unacceptable. When left unacknowledged, they understand these hidden elements can hinder spiritual growth and lead to disharmony within the self. The process of shadow integration begins with the courageous act of shining the light of awareness into the darker corners of the psyche.

As the voyager delves into shadow work, they discover the transformative power of self-compassion and forgiveness. These qualities become vital tools in the integration journey, allowing the seeker to approach their shadow with kindness and understanding rather than judgment or fear.

Once integrated, the sojourner finds that the shadow reveals invaluable gifts and strengths. Traits and potentials, once buried beneath layers of denial or shame, emerge as sources of power and authenticity, enriching the seeker's journey and enhancing their capacity to connect with others.

In the dance of shadow and light, the pilgrim learns the art of balance. They recognize that neither aspect can exist without the other and that the interplay between them gives rise to the full spectrum of human experience. This balance fosters inner peace and wholeness, grounding the seeker in their true essence.

The pathfinder encounters the collective shadow in their journey, witnessing how societal and cultural shadows manifest in the world around them. They understand that personal shadow work is intrinsically linked to the healing of collective wounds, contributing to the evolution of consciousness globally.

Through integration, the wanderer discovers the alchemical potential of the shadow. They learn that by transmuting the shadow's energy through understanding and acceptance, they can transform their deepest fears and challenges into catalysts for spiritual awakening and growth.

The nomad realizes that integrating shadow and light is an ongoing process, not a destination. Each stage of life brings new opportunities for self-discovery and transformation, inviting the seeker to explore the depths and heights of their being continually.

The odyssey of integrating shadow and light teaches the seeker that true enlightenment encompasses the entirety of the self. By embracing both the shadow and the light, the seeker steps into a more authentic and empowered expression of their being, radiating wholeness and harmony.

Finally, the adept sees that the integration of shadow and light is a profound act of love—love for oneself, others, and life's journey. This act of love propels the seeker forward on the path to enlightenment, guiding them toward a state of unity and oneness with all that is.

In the heart-expanding journey toward enlightenment, the seeker embraces the transformative virtues of compassion and altruism. This path illuminates the intrinsic connection between the well-being of the self and the well-being of others, revealing that true spiritual awakening is deeply intertwined with the acts of understanding, empathizing with, and serving others.

The adept discovers that compassion is not merely an emotion but a state of being, a way of relating to all living beings with kindness, understanding, and a deep recognition of their inherent interconnectedness. This compassionate stance becomes the bedrock upon which they build their interactions and decisions, coloring their journey with empathy and care.

As the wanderer delves deeper into the practice of compassion, they encounter the concept of bodhicitta in the Buddhist tradition—the noble intention to achieve enlightenment for the sake of all beings. This aspiration becomes a guiding light for the seeker, inspiring them to transcend personal liberation and work towards alleviating suffering in the world.

The pilgrim learns that altruism—the selfless concern for the welfare of others—expands their sense of self beyond the confines of individualism. Through acts of generosity, service, and kindness, the seeker experiences a profound sense of connection and unity with the tapestry of life, enhancing their spiritual growth and understanding of fulfillment.

In the dance of compassion and altruism, the voyager recognizes the healing power of these virtues. They see how extending compassion to others and engaging in charitable acts uplifts those they help and heals and transforms their heart, dissolving barriers and opening channels of love and light.

The traveler finds that compassion and altruism are nurtured through practices such as loving-kindness meditation (Metta), selfless service (Seva), and the cultivation of an open heart. These practices deepen the seeker's capacity for empathy and self-giving, anchoring their spiritual journey in the principles of love and service.

Through their commitment to compassion and altruism, the nomad becomes a beacon of hope and comfort to those around them. Their presence and actions create ripples of kindness and understanding, contributing to a collective elevation of consciousness and a more compassionate world.

The pathfinder encounters the wisdom that genuine compassion includes oneself. They learn the importance of self-compassion, treating themselves with the same kindness and understanding they offer others. This self-compassion is crucial for maintaining balance and preventing burnout, ensuring that the seeker's well of compassion remains replenished.

In their exploration, the sojourner realizes that compassion and altruism transcend cultural, religious, and ideological boundaries. These universal virtues are celebrated across spiritual traditions, highlighting their central role in the human quest for meaning and connection.

Finally, the adept understands that cultivating compassion and altruism is an endless journey that continually challenges and enriches them. By placing compassion and altruism at the heart of their spiritual practice, the seeker advances on their path to enlightenment and contributes to the awakening and healing of the world, embodying the true essence of enlightened living.

In the profound odyssey towards enlightenment, the adept undertakes the challenging yet liberating task of transcending the ego and cultivating humility. This journey unveils the ego's illusory nature and its role in perpetuating separation and suffering, guiding the seeker toward realizing a more expansive, interconnected sense of self grounded in humility and unity.

The pilgrim understands that the ego, with its desires, fears, and attachments, often operates as a barrier to spiritual awakening. By recognizing the ego's transient and illusory nature, the seeker begins loosening its grip, opening the gateway to deeper levels of consciousness and connection.

As the wanderer explores the landscape of humility, they discover its power to dissolve the ego's boundaries, fostering a sense of oneness with all life. Humility becomes not a sign of weakness but a testament to the seeker's strength and wisdom, revealing their proper place within the vast tapestry of existence.

The traveler learns that transcending the ego involves a continuous practice of self-observation and awareness. Mindfully witnessing their thoughts, emotions, and actions without identification, the seeker gradually disentangles their essence from the ego's narratives, finding freedom in this detachment.

In the cultivation of humility, the voyager embraces the practice of service to others as a pathway to ego transcendence. Through selfless service, the seeker experiences the dissolution of egoic boundaries, expanding their sense of self to include the well-being of others and the collective whole.

The nomad finds that moments of awe and wonder, often inspired by nature's majesty or the arts, provide potent antidotes to the ego's confinement. These experiences of transcendence remind the seeker of their smallness in the face of the universe's vastness, nurturing a natural humility and reverence for life.

Through their journey, the sojourner encounters the wisdom of spiritual teachers and traditions, highlighting the ego's role as a teacher rather than an enemy. By understanding and integrating the ego's lessons, the seeker transforms their relationship with it, using its challenges to fuel growth and awakening.

The pathfinder realizes that humility is not about self-deprecation but about recognizing one's inherent worth and acknowledging the interconnectedness and equality of all beings. This balanced perspective fosters genuine self-esteem and respect for others, grounded in recognizing the divine spark within every soul.

In their quest, the adept learn that transcending the ego and cultivating humility are not one-time achievements but ongoing processes. Each moment presents an opportunity to choose humility over ego, compassion over judgment, and unity over separation, deepening the seeker's embodiment of enlightened principles.

Finally, the seeker understands that the journey beyond the ego and into the heart of humility is one of the most profound paths to enlightenment. By embracing this path, the adept not only liberates themselves from the confines of egoic illusion but also becomes a luminous example of the peace, love, and unity that characterize an enlightened life, inspiring others to embark on their journey of transcendence and awakening.

The adept attests to the subtle yet profound phenomena of synchronicity and divine timing in the intricate dance toward enlightenment. This exploration delves into the meaningful coincidences and perfectly orchestrated moments that defy mere chance, guiding the seeker toward a more profound understanding and alignment with the universe's flow.

The explorer discerns that synchronicities are not random occurrences, but signals from the universe breadcrumbs on the path to awakening that affirm the seeker's direction or offer insight. These serendipitous events are recognized as manifestations of the interconnected web of existence, where all elements are in constant, harmonious communication.

As the wanderer attunes to the rhythm of divine timing, they learn the art of patience and trust. They understand their spiritual journey unfolds according to a cosmic schedule transcending personal desires and timelines. This trust in divine timing cultivates a deep sense of peace and surrender, freeing the seeker from the anxiety of 'when' and 'how.'

The pilgrim discovers that synchronicity and divine timing often emerge most clearly in moments of stillness and presence. By quieting the mind and attuning to the present moment, the seeker opens themselves to the subtle whispers of the universe, becoming receptive to its guidance and wisdom.

In their journey, the voyager finds that embracing synchronicity and divine timing requires an open heart and mind. By remaining fluid and adaptable, the seeker allows themselves to be led by the universe's signs, even when they deviate from preconceived plans or expectations.

The traveler learns that synchronicities often affirm the seeker's intuitions and inner knowing. These meaningful coincidences reinforce the seeker's trust in their inner guidance, strengthening their confidence in navigating the spiritual path with autonomy and assurance.

Through their attunement to synchronicity and divine timing, the nomad experiences a deepening faith in the unseen forces guiding and shaping their journey. This faith transcends intellectual understanding, rooting the seeker in a heartfelt recognition of the divine orchestration in all aspects of life.

The sojourner appreciates that synchronicity and divine timing are expressions of the universe's benevolence, designed to support the seeker's evolution and enlightenment. Each synchronistic event and instance of divine timing is a gift imbued with love and tailored to the seeker's unique path.

In their contemplation, the adept realize that synchronicity and divine timing are not merely external phenomena but reflections of the seeker's inner alignment with the universe. As the seeker harmonizes their being with the cosmic flow, they become co-creators in the tapestry of existence, weaving their destiny in partnership with the divine.

Finally, the seeker understands that the dance with synchronicity and divine timing is integral to the spiritual journey, offering continual opportunities for growth, confirmation, and wonder. By embracing these divine winks, the seeker deepens their connection with the universe, moving gracefully along the path to enlightenment with a sense of awe, gratitude, and divine timing guiding their way.

In the sacred journey towards enlightenment, the seeker embraces the profound teaching of impermanence, recognizing the transient nature of all things. This acceptance opens the heart to the flowing rhythm of existence, allowing the seeker to move with grace and resilience through the ever-changing tapestry of life.

The traveler learns that impermanence is not a cause for despair but a gateway to freedom. Acknowledging the fleeting nature of experiences, relationships, and material conditions, the seeker is liberated from attachment and aversion, finding peace in the continuous dance of creation and dissolution.

As the wanderer contemplates the ebb and flow of life, they discover the beauty in transience. Each moment, with its unique configuration of elements, becomes precious and sacred, imbued with a poignancy that enriches the seeker's journey with depth and meaning.

The pilgrim finds solace in the cycles of nature, where impermanence is the fundamental principle governing all life. The changing seasons, the waxing and waning of the moon, and the life cycles of beings reflect the inherent wisdom of impermanence, teaching the seeker to honor the rhythms of birth, growth, decay, and renewal.

In the realm of impermanence, the voyager cultivates a heart of serenity. They learn to greet joy and sorrow, gain and loss, with the same steady composure, understanding that all experiences are transient waves on the ocean of consciousness, neither to be clung to nor rejected.

The nomad embraces the practice of mindfulness as a means to engage fully with the impermanent nature of the present moment. Through mindful awareness, the seeker deepens their appreciation for the impermanent beauty of the now, living each moment entirely and without reservation.

Through their acceptance of impermanence, the explorer is guided to live with intention and purpose. Recognizing that time is a precious and finite resource, the seeker becomes deliberate in their choices, actions, and pursuits, aligning their life with their deepest values and aspirations.

The sojourner discovers that embracing impermanence fosters a spirit of adaptability and resilience. They become adept at navigating change, turning challenges into opportunities for growth, and gracefully letting go of what no longer serves their highest good.

In their reflection on impermanence, the adept uncovers a paradoxical truth: within the heart of transience lies a doorway to the eternal. By fully embracing the impermanent nature of the phenomenal world, the seeker touches the timeless essence that underlies all forms, finding a wellspring of enduring peace and stability amidst the flux.

Finally, the seeker realizes that embracing impermanence is a profound spiritual practice that illuminates the path to enlightenment. By living in harmony with the flow of life, the seeker embodies the wisdom of impermanence, becoming a testament to the grace, flexibility, and open-heartedness that characterize an enlightened existence.

In the rich tapestry of the spiritual journey, the seeker delves into the transformative world of sacred rituals and ceremonies. These ancient practices, steeped in symbolism and intention, serve as portals to the divine, connecting the seeker to the deeper currents of spiritual energy and universal wisdom.

The pilgrim discovers that rituals and ceremonies are not mere formalities but acts of co-creation with the divine. Through these sacred practices, the seeker actively engages with the spiritual realm, invoking the presence of higher energies and aligning themselves with cosmic forces, thereby weaving their intentions into the fabric of reality.

As the voyager explores various traditions, they encounter myriad rituals and ceremonies, each with its unique symbols, rites, and purposes. From the meditative calm of a tea ceremony to the vibrant energy of a drum circle, the seeker learns to appreciate the diverse ways humanity connects with the sacred.

The adept learns that the power of rituals lies in their ability to consecrate time and space, creating a sanctified environment where the mundane world is transcended and the sacred is palpably present. In these consecrated spaces, the seeker finds a deep sense of peace, clarity, and connection to all that is.

Through participation in rituals, the traveler cultivates a sense of community and shared purpose. Whether in solitary practice or group ceremonies, the seeker experiences the strength and support of collective intention, amplifying the spiritual energy and fostering a sense of unity and belonging.

The sojourner understands that rituals and ceremonies are vehicles for marking life's transitions and milestones. From birth to death and all the pivotal moments in between, these sacred practices honor the soul's journey, acknowledging growth, change, and the passage of time.

In their engagement with ritual, the wanderer discovers the healing power of these ancient practices. Through purification rites, healing ceremonies, or release rituals, the seeker finds restoration and renewal, shedding old energies and embracing new beginnings.

The nomad realizes that creating personal rituals is a powerful expression of their spiritual path. By crafting ceremonies that resonate with their inner being, the seeker imbues their practice with deep personal meaning, strengthening their connection to the divine in a way that is uniquely their own.

The explorer taps into the wellspring of ancestral wisdom through sacred rituals and ceremonies. They recognize that these practices are spiritual acts and bridges to the past, connecting the seeker to the lineage of seekers, shamans, and mystics who have walked the path before them.

Finally, the seeker understands that the power of sacred rituals and ceremonies lies in transforming the ordinary into the extraordinary, infusing the seeker's life with a sense of wonder, reverence, and deep spiritual connection. By integrating these sacred practices into their journey, the seeker weaves a rich, meaningful tapestry of spiritual experience anchored in the timeless traditions that have guided humanity's quest for the divine.

In the profound quest for enlightenment, the seeker turns inward, cultivating the sacred realms of inner silence and deep listening. This introspective journey reveals the subtle whispers of the soul and the universe, guiding the seeker toward profound insights and a more intimate communion with the divine.

The adept learns inner silence is more than the absence of noise; it is a vibrant state of being where the mind's constant chatter is transcended, revealing the luminous landscape of the seeker's true essence. In this sanctuary of stillness, the seeker encounters the depths of their wisdom and the gentle guidance of the spiritual realm.

As the voyager cultivates inner silence, they discover the power of deep listening—the ability to hear not only with the ears but with the heart and soul. This form of listening attunes the seeker to the subtle frequencies of intuition, the silent language of nature, and the unspoken truths that permeate the cosmos.

The pilgrim finds that meditation is a key to unlocking inner silence and the power of listening. Through disciplined stillness and focused attention, the seeker learns to quiet the mind and attune to the vastness of their inner world, where the voice of the divine softly speaks.

In embracing inner silence, the traveler realizes the transformative impact of listening to their body. The seeker becomes attuned to the body's wisdom, listening to its needs, messages, and signals, fostering a harmonious balance between physical well-being and spiritual growth.

The sojourner discovers inner silence and deep listening enhance their connections. By listening from a place of stillness and presence, the seeker engages in more meaningful and empathetic interactions, fostering deeper relationships and a greater sense of kinship with all beings.

Through their journey into silence, the nomad encounters the paradox that one finds the most profound answers in silence. The questions that once seemed impossible are met with clarity and insight in the serenity of the seeker's soul, where the universe itself offers guidance and solace.

The wanderer learns to integrate moments of silence into daily life, recognizing that inner silence is not confined to meditation or solitary retreats but can be a constant companion, offering peace and clarity amidst the bustle of the everyday world.

In cultivating the power of listening, the adept becomes a student of life, open to the lessons and wisdom that each moment, each encounter, and each challenge brings. This openness transforms the seeker's journey into a rich tapestry of learning and discovery, guided by the quiet voice of truth that speaks within.

Finally, the seeker understands that the cultivation of inner silence and the power of listening are essential practices on the path to enlightenment. By fostering these sacred qualities, the seeker deepens their spiritual journey and becomes a beacon of peace, understanding, and wisdom in a world that yearns for the transformative power of silence and genuine listening.

In the unfolding tapestry of the spiritual quest, the seeker embraces enlightenment not as a finite destination but as an infinite journey of continuous growth, discovery, and expansion. This realization illuminates the path with a sense of dynamism and adventure, where each step, each insight, and each moment of awakening contributes to an ever-deepening understanding of the self and the cosmos.

The pilgrim recognizes that enlightenment is a multifaceted prism, revealing new colors and dimensions with every perspective turn. This understanding encourages the seeker to remain open and fluid, allowing their conception of enlightenment to evolve with their experiences and insights.

As the voyager traverses this endless journey, they discover that enlightenment is woven into the fabric of daily life. The mundane and the sacred merge, revealing that moments of illumination can arise in the simplest of activities, transforming the ordinary into a living meditation.

The adept learns that enlightenment is marked by cycles of ebb and flow. Periods of profound insight and connection are interspersed with times of challenge and introspection, each phase offering unique lessons and growth opportunities.

In the seeker's heart, there grows an appreciation for the companions who share the path. The journey is enriched by fellow travelers' wisdom, support, and camaraderie, each contributing their light to the collective quest for understanding and awakening.

The wanderer understands that obstacles and setbacks are integral to the enlightenment journey. Each hurdle is an invitation to delve deeper, to confront and transcend personal limitations, and to emerge with greater resilience and wisdom.

Through the infinite journey, the sojourner embraces the role of the eternal student, humbly acknowledging that there is always more to learn, unlearn, and discover. This humble approach keeps the seeker's heart and mind open to new teachings, experiences, and revelations.

The nomad finds joy in the journey itself, recognizing that the pursuit of enlightenment is not just about attaining a transcendent state but about the richness of the journey. The path becomes a tapestry of moments to be cherished, lessons to be learned, and mysteries to be explored.

In their contemplation, the traveler realizes that enlightenment is more about serving others than personal awakening. The journey expands to include acts of kindness, compassion, and service, understanding that each act of love and generosity lights the way for all.

Finally, the seeker sees the infinite journey of enlightenment as the ultimate expression of life's beauty and complexity. Embracing the journey in its entirety, with all its twists and turns, the seeker walks the path with a heart full of wonder, a mind open to the endless horizons of understanding, and a spirit attuned to the timeless dance of becoming.

Chapter 9:

In the continuous journey of spiritual growth, the seeker embarks on the profound task of integrating spirituality into the fabric of daily life. This path unveils the transformative practice of mindfulness, revealing how each moment offers an opportunity for presence, awareness, and connection to the deeper currents of existence.

The pilgrim discovers that mindfulness is the art of being fully present with one's experiences, observing thoughts, emotions, and sensations without judgment. This practice illuminates the richness of ordinary moments, transforming mundane activities into gateways to the sacred.

As the voyager cultivates mindfulness, they learn to navigate the ebb and flow of daily life with grace and poise. The challenges and stresses of the everyday world become less overwhelming, met with a centered calm that stems from a deep well of inner peace.

The adept finds that mindfulness enriches relationships, allowing deeper connections and more authentic interactions. By being fully present with others, the seeker fosters a sense of openness, empathy, and understanding, enhancing the quality of their connections.

In work and responsibilities, the seeker applies mindfulness to their tasks, finding focus and efficiency. This intentional approach to work transforms it from a source of stress to a form of service and a means of spiritual practice.

The wayfarer integrates mindfulness into self-care routines, recognizing the body as a temple of the spirit. Eating, exercising, and resting are approached with reverence and intention, nurturing physical and spiritual well-being.

Through mindfulness, the traveler becomes attuned to the beauty and wonder of the natural world. Simple pleasures like the warmth of sunlight, the sound of rain, or the scent of flowers become profound experiences, reminding the seeker of the interconnectedness of all life.

The nomad learns that mindfulness is a key to resilience, providing the strength to face life's adversities with courage and insight. Challenges are met with a mindful awareness that fosters learning and growth, transforming obstacles into opportunities for spiritual development.

In their practice of mindfulness, the sojourner discovers the power of gratitude. Each moment becomes an occasion for thankfulness, cultivating a heart open to joy, wonder, and the universe's abundance.

Finally, the seeker realizes that mindfulness is a practice and a way of life. By integrating mindfulness into every aspect of their daily existence, the seeker embodies the essence of spirituality in action, transforming their life into a living meditation, a continuous celebration of the present moment and the divine presence that permeates all.

In the ongoing evolution of the spiritual path, the seeker turns their attention to the art of conscious communication and the cultivation of meaningful relationships. This journey emphasizes the power of words and interactions to build bridges of understanding, empathy, and deep connection with oneself and others.

The adept learns that conscious communication begins with deep, attentive, open-hearted listening that seeks to understand rather than respond. This quality of listening allows the seeker to truly hear the words and feelings of others, fostering a space of trust and openness.

As the voyager explores the dynamics of conscious communication, they discover the importance of mindfulness in speech. They strive to speak truthfully, kindly, and constructively, recognizing that their words have the power to heal or harm. This mindful approach to communication transforms conversations into acts of compassion and connection.

The pilgrim finds that relationships are mirrors, reflecting aspects of the self that need attention, healing, or growth. Through conscious communication, the seeker engages with these reflections in a way that promotes self-awareness and mutual understanding, deepening the bonds of intimacy and friendship.

In conflict and disagreement, the seeker applies the principles of conscious communication to navigate differences with respect and grace. They learn the art of assertiveness—expressing their needs and boundaries clearly and respectfully while honoring the perspectives of others.

The wayfarer cultivates the practice of empathy, striving to see the world through the eyes of others. This empathetic engagement allows the seeker to connect on a profound level, transcending barriers of judgment and fostering a sense of shared humanity.

Through conscious communication, the traveler emphasizes the power of vulnerability. By sharing their authentic self, including fears and uncertainties, the seeker invites others to do the same, creating relationships that are rich in authenticity and mutual support.

The nomad recognizes that conscious communication is not limited to words. They become attuned to the subtleties of body language, tone of voice, and energetic exchange, understanding that accurate communication encompasses the entire being.

In their journey, the adept learns that conscious communication is a pathway to spiritual community. By engaging with others in a spirit of openness and sincerity, the seeker builds a network of spiritual allies—fellow travelers who provide support, inspiration, and companionship on the path.

Finally, the seeker understands that conscious communication and relationships are fundamental to the spiritual journey. By cultivating these practices, the seeker enriches their path and creates a more compassionate, understanding, and connected world. Through conscious communication, the seeker weaves a tapestry of relationships that uplift, inspire, and illuminate the path to enlightenment.

In the enriching journey of spiritual living, the seeker embarks on the transformative path of blending spiritual practices with their work and creative expressions. This exploration reveals how one's vocational and artistic endeavors can become a profound medium for spiritual growth, service, and expressing one's most profound truths.

The adept discovers that work transcends mere economic activity when approached as a form of spiritual practice. They learn to infuse their daily tasks with mindfulness, presence, and a sense of sacred purpose, transforming routine duties into acts of meditation and devotion.

As the wanderer delves into the realm of creativity, they find it a powerful conduit for spiritual expression and exploration. Through art, writing, music, or any creative endeavor, the seeker realizes that creativity can mirror the soul, reflecting and exploring the depths of their spiritual journey.

The pilgrim learns the importance of intention in integrating spirituality into work and creativity. By setting clear, heartfelt intentions, the seeker aligns their efforts with their spiritual values and aspirations, ensuring that their work and creative outputs contribute to their evolution and the greater good.

In integrating spirituality with work, the voyager sees challenges and obstacles as opportunities for spiritual learning and growth. Difficulties in the workplace become lessons in patience, resilience, and compassion, deepening the seeker's spiritual maturity and understanding.

The traveler explores the "right livelihood" concept, seeking alignment between their vocational path and spiritual principles. They strive to engage in work that meets their material needs, resonates with their ethical values, and contributes positively to the world.

The nomad embraces collaboration and teamwork as a spiritual practice, recognizing the divine in each colleague and partner. The seeker fosters a work environment that reflects spiritual principles and nurtures collective growth by cultivating empathy, respect, and open-hearted communication.

Through their creative expressions, the seeker finds a unique voice for their spiritual insights and revelations. Creativity becomes a sacred dialogue with the divine, a way to explore and share the mysteries of the spiritual path with others, inviting viewers, readers, or listeners into their reflective journey.

The adept understands that integrating spirituality into work and creativity requires a balance between effort and surrender. They learn to give their best while remaining detached from the outcomes, trusting in the flow of divine will and the inherent value of the creative process itself.

Finally, the seeker realizes that integrating spiritual practices into work and creativity is an ongoing discovery, refinement, and alignment journey. By continually seeking ways to infuse their vocational and creative pursuits with spiritual depth, the seeker enriches their own life and serves as a beacon of inspiration and transformation in the world, illustrating how work and creativity can be vibrant expressions of the spiritual heart.

In the expansive journey of spiritual integration, the seeker turns their gaze outward, focusing on the potent role of service and contribution in fostering spiritual growth. This path illuminates the profound truth that true enlightenment blossoms not just through inward reflection but also through acts of kindness, generosity, and commitment to the welfare of others.

The adept learns that service is a natural expression of the spiritual self, a tangible manifestation of the interconnectedness of all life. By contributing to the well-being of others, the seeker transcends the boundaries of the ego, experiencing firsthand the joy and fulfillment that come from selfless giving.

As the wanderer engages in acts of service, they discover the diversity of forms service can take. Whether volunteering for a cause, offering support to a friend, or engaging in advocacy for social change, each act of service is imbued with spiritual significance, transforming the giver as much as the recipient.

The pilgrim finds that contribution to the community is a moral or ethical duty and a spiritual practice that enriches the giver's soul. This realization deepens the seeker's commitment to service, viewing it as an essential component of their spiritual path and a powerful vehicle for personal transformation.

In service, the voyager learns the importance of empathy and compassion. These virtues guide the seeker's actions, ensuring their contributions are sensitive, respectful, and responsive to the actual needs of those they serve, fostering a genuine connection and mutual growth.

The traveler explores the concept of "karma yoga," the yoga of selfless action, which teaches that service performed without attachment to the results purifies the heart and leads to spiritual liberation. This principle encourages the seeker to approach service with humility and openness, free from the desire for recognition or reward.

Through service and contribution, the nomad experiences the dissolution of the illusion of separation between self and others. This realization of oneness is a cornerstone of spiritual awakening, revealing that in serving others, the seeker is, in truth, serving the divine essence that resides in all.

The adept finds that integrating service into daily life requires mindfulness and intentionality. They seek opportunities to serve in everyday interactions and tasks, embodying the spirit of service in all aspects of life, from the grand to the mundane.

In their journey, the sojourner discovers that giving and contributing is also a process of receiving. Through service, the seeker gets lessons in love, gratitude, humility, and the boundless capacity of the human spirit to overcome adversity and manifest beauty.

Finally, the seeker understands that fostering spiritual growth through service and contribution is an ever-evolving practice. As they continue to serve, their actions become increasingly aligned with the highest principles of love, compassion, and unity. Through this alignment, the seeker not only advances on their spiritual path but also contributes to the healing and upliftment of the world, affirming that service is a profound expression of the enlightened heart.

In the ever-evolving journey of life, the seeker is called to cultivate spiritual resilience, an inner strength that enables one to navigate the winds of change with grace, faith, and unwavering calm. This exploration delves into the heart of adaptability, revealing how the spiritual path equips the voyager with the tools to face uncertainty and transformation with a centered and open heart.

The adept learns that spiritual resilience is rooted in a deep trust in the universe and its plan. By surrendering to the flow of life, the seeker finds strength not in resistance but in the ability to move with change, seeing it as an opportunity for growth and deeper understanding.

As the wanderer embraces the concept of impermanence, they discover the liberating truth that all things pass, yet the essence remains. This understanding allows the seeker to face loss and transition with a sense of peace, knowing that each ending is also a beginning and each challenges a doorway to new possibilities.

The pilgrim finds solace in their spiritual practices during times of change. Whether through meditation, prayer, or contemplation, these practices become anchors, stabilizing the seeker amid life's storms and reminding them of the constant presence of the divine.

In cultivating spiritual resilience, the voyager learns the power of perspective. They recognize that their reaction to change is a choice and that by viewing events through a lens of spiritual insight, they can transform adversity into a catalyst for awakening and transformation.

The traveler discovers that community and spiritual companionship are invaluable resources in building resilience. The seeker gains support, wisdom, and strength from shared experience and collective faith by sharing their journey with like-minded souls.

Through the journey of change, the nomad develops a profound inner flexibility. This adaptability allows the seeker to embrace new situations and altered circumstances with curiosity and openness, free from the constraints of past expectations and rigid self-identities.

The adept realizes that gratitude plays a crucial role in cultivating resilience. The seeker fosters a positive outlook that fuels their inner strength and capacity to overcome challenges by focusing on each moment's blessings, even in times of hardship.

In their exploration, the sojourner learns that spiritual resilience is an ongoing practice. It requires continuous nurturing through reflection, self-care, and reaffirming trust in the journey. This dedication ensures that the seeker's spirit remains buoyant, able to rise above the transient waves of change.

Finally, the seeker understands that cultivating spiritual resilience in times of change is a personal triumph and a gift to the world. By embodying resilience, the seeker becomes a beacon of hope and stability, inspiring others to find their inner strength and to face life's uncertainties with courage, compassion, and an open heart.

In the unfolding journey of spiritual integration, the seeker turns to the nurturing practice of gratitude, discovering its transformative power to expand the heart, soul, and perception of life. This exploration delves into how a sustained attitude of thankfulness catalyzes profound spiritual growth and an enriched experience of existence.

The adept finds that gratitude is more than a fleeting sentiment; it is a profound recognition of the abundance and blessings permeating every aspect of life. By focusing on the gifts present in each moment, the seeker shifts from a mindset of scarcity to one of abundance, opening their heart to the infinite generosity of the universe.

As the wanderer cultivates a daily gratitude practice, they notice a significant shift in their interactions with the world. Challenges and obstacles are met with a more profound sense of calm and perspective as the seeker learns to find the silver lining and lessons within every situation.

The pilgrim discovers that gratitude deepens their connection to the divine. In recognizing the source of all blessings, the seeker's relationship with the spiritual realm is strengthened, fostering a sense of closeness and communion with the sacred.

In the practice of gratitude, the voyager learns to appreciate the beauty of the present moment. This appreciation brings a richness to life that transcends material possessions or external achievements, revealing the inherent value and sanctity of the now.

The traveler finds that gratitude is a key to unlocking joy and contentment. By celebrating what they have, rather than lamenting what they lack, the seeker experiences a profound joy that is not contingent on external circumstances but flows from an internal wellspring.

Through their engagement with gratitude, the nomad realizes its power to heal and transform relationships. Expressing appreciation and recognizing the contributions of others nurtures mutual respect and love, healing old wounds and building bridges of understanding.

The adept learns that gratitude is an antidote to ego and entitlement. By acknowledging that every blessing is a gift and not a given, the seeker cultivates humility and a genuine sense of appreciation for the myriad ways life supports and enriches their journey.

In their reflection, the sojourner understands that gratitude fosters resilience. Armed with thankfulness, the seeker is better equipped to navigate life's ups and downs, maintaining a positive outlook and an open heart, even in the face of adversity.

Finally, the seeker sees gratitude as an essential practice in the spiritual journey, expanding the soul and aligning the individual with the vibrational frequency of abundance, love, and unity. By embedding gratitude into the fabric of daily life, the seeker not only enriches their own experience but also contributes to the collective upliftment of humanity, radiating the transformative power of thankfulness in every thought, word, and action.1

In the profound journey of spiritual living, the seeker embarks on the deeply healing path of forgiveness. This exploration uncovers the transformative power of releasing old wounds, grievances, and resentments, highlighting how forgiveness is an act of benevolence towards others and a pivotal step towards personal freedom and spiritual expansion.

The adept learns that forgiveness is an act of strength and courage, requiring the seeker to confront and release the pain of the past. This process is not about condoning hurtful actions but about liberating the heart from the chains of bitterness, allowing space for peace and renewal.

As the wanderer delves into the practice of forgiveness, they discover its capacity to heal emotional wounds and mend the fabric of relationships. Forgiving others opens the door to reconciliation and deeper connections built on the foundations of understanding and compassion.

The pilgrim finds that self-forgiveness is an essential aspect of this transformative journey. The seeker acknowledges their mistakes and shortcomings, extending their compassion and understanding to themselves as they would to others. This act of self-forgiveness paves the way for self-acceptance and growth.

In the realm of forgiveness, the voyager learns the power of empathy and perspective-taking. By endeavoring to see situations from the viewpoint of others, the seeker gains insights into the motivations and circumstances that lead to hurtful actions, facilitating a deeper understanding and fostering forgiveness.

The traveler discovers that forgiveness is a key to unlocking spiritual insights. By releasing old grievances, the seeker's heart and mind are opened to higher truths and deeper connections with the divine, unobstructed by the weight of unresolved anger and resentment.

Through their engagement with forgiveness, the nomad realizes its role in breaking cycles of negativity and pain. Forgiveness is the force that halts the perpetuation of suffering, transforming personal and collective karma through the alchemy of love and compassion.

The adept finds that forgiveness requires patience and persistence. It is often a process rather than a one-time act, involving layers of hurt that need time and intention to heal fully. The seeker learns to trust this process, allowing forgiveness to unfold in its own time and way.

In their journey, the sojourner witnesses the liberating effect of forgiveness on the spirit. Freed from the burdens of the past, the seeker experiences a profound lightness of being, enabling them to move forward on their spiritual path with greater ease and joy.

Finally, the seeker comes to understand that harnessing the transformative power of forgiveness is a profound spiritual practice, one that enriches the soul and elevates the collective consciousness. By embracing forgiveness, the seeker not only heals themselves but also contributes to the healing of the world, radiating the vibrations of reconciliation, peace, and unconditional love.

One is also to remember that forgiveness is a process that involves overtime. Does not happen with a snap of the fingers.

In the rich tapestry of spiritual integration, the seeker embarks on the essential practice of living with intention, a conscious journey of aligning every thought, word, and action with their deepest spiritual values. This exploration reveals the power of intentionality in crafting a life that reflects the seeker's highest aspirations and serves as a beacon of light and transformation in the world.

The adept discovers that living with intention begins with clarity about one's core spiritual values and principles. By identifying these guiding lights, the seeker sets the foundation for a life directed by purpose and enriched with meaning, ensuring that their daily choices resonate with their soul's true calling.

As the wanderer cultivates the art of intentionality, they learn to pause and reflect before acting, asking themselves whether their impending actions align with their spiritual ethos. This mindful approach transforms decision-making into a sacred practice, imbuing the simplest choices with significance and depth.

The pilgrim finds that living with intention enhances their awareness of the present moment. By focusing on the here and now, the seeker ensures that their actions are deliberate and focused rather than reactive or unconscious, thereby deepening their engagement with life and the divine.

In intentionality, the voyager embraces the practice of setting daily intentions. Each morning, the seeker affirms their commitment to living according to their spiritual values, setting the tone for the day and guiding their interactions and activities towards higher purposes.

The traveler discovers the power of intention in manifesting spiritual goals and visions. By holding a clear and focused intention, the seeker aligns their energy with their aspirations, attracting the circumstances, resources, and connections needed to bring their spiritual visions to fruition.

Through their journey, the nomad learns that living with intention requires flexibility and openness to divine guidance. The seeker remains receptive to the universe's signs and nudges, understanding that accurate alignment sometimes calls for adaptation and trust in the higher plan.

The adept realizes that intentionality extends beyond personal growth to include the welfare of others and the planet. By aligning their actions with values of compassion, service, and stewardship, the seeker contributes to the collective upliftment and healing of the world, embodying the principles of interconnectedness and love.

In living with intention, the sojourner experiences a deepening sense of fulfillment and peace. Knowing that their life is aligned with their spiritual values brings a profound satisfaction that transcends external achievements or recognition, anchoring the seeker in a sense of purpose and joy.

Finally, the seeker understands that living with intention is an ongoing journey of refinement and discovery. As they continue to align their actions with their spiritual values, the seeker not only navigates the path of personal transformation but also inspires others to consider the transformative power of intentionality in their own lives, fostering a world where actions are guided by the heart's most profound truths and the spirit's boundless aspirations.

In the holistic journey of spiritual integration, the seeker explores the interconnectedness of physical, mental, emotional, and spiritual health. This exploration brings to light the profound understanding that true well-being transcends the physical realm, necessitating a balanced and comprehensive approach that nurtures every facet of the human experience.

The adept learns that holistic health begins with recognizing the body as a sacred vessel for the spirit. By honoring their physical form through nutritious food, regular exercise, and sufficient rest, the seeker sets a strong foundation for their spiritual practices, acknowledging that a vibrant body supports a lively spirit.

As the wanderer delves into health's mental and emotional dimensions, they discover the importance of mindfulness, positive thinking, and emotional resilience. Cultivating a peaceful mind and a harmonious emotional landscape becomes essential to their daily routine, contributing to well-being and spiritual clarity.

The pilgrim finds that spiritual health is the cornerstone of holistic well-being. Regular spiritual practices such as meditation, prayer, or contemplation allow the seeker to connect with their innermost self and the divine, fostering a deep sense of peace, purpose, and interconnectedness with all life.

In the quest for holistic health, the voyager explores the healing power of nature. Immersing themselves in the natural world, the seeker finds restoration and rejuvenation, reminded of the earth's innate wisdom and healing rhythms that mirror the seeker's journey toward wholeness.

The traveler learns the value of relationships and community in nurturing well-being. Surrounding themselves with supportive and like-minded individuals provides a network of care, inspiration, and shared growth, reinforcing the seeker's commitment to holistic health and spiritual expansion.

Through their journey, the nomad discovers the significance of self-care and self-compassion. Recognizing their own needs and treating themselves with kindness and understanding becomes a spiritual act, affirming their worth and fostering a loving relationship with themselves.

The adept realizes that holistic health involves an ongoing process of self-discovery and adjustment. By tuning into their body, mind, and spirit, the seeker learns to identify imbalances and address them with appropriate practices, ensuring that their approach to well-being evolves with their changing needs and insights.

In their exploration, the sojourner encounters various holistic modalities and therapies that complement their spiritual practice. From acupuncture and yoga to herbal medicine and energy healing, the seeker remains open to integrating diverse healing practices that resonate with their path and enhance their overall well-being.

Finally, the seeker understands that embracing a holistic approach to health and well-being is integral to the spiritual path. By nurturing their entire being, the seeker advances on their journey towards enlightenment and becomes a testament to the transformative power of living in harmony with the body, mind, and spirit, inspiring others to explore the profound depths of holistic health.

In the spiritual journey of integration and embodiment, the seeker extends their focus beyond personal transformation to include nurturing peace and harmony in their environment. This exploration underlines the profound interconnectedness between the seeker's inner state and the external world, revealing how cultivating a sacred space can be a powerful extension of one's spiritual practice.

The adept recognizes that our spaces—our homes, workplaces, and natural surroundings—hold significant energy that influences our well-being and spiritual vibrancy. By consciously creating environments that reflect peace, beauty, and harmony, the seeker fosters a conducive setting for spiritual growth and inner tranquility.

As the wayfarer embarks on the practice of environmental harmony, they learn the art of space clearing and energy cleansing. Techniques such as smudging with sage, sound clearing with bells or singing bowls, and using crystals become tools in purifying and elevating the energy of their surroundings, making them resonate with higher vibrational frequencies.

The pilgrim discovers the power of sacred objects and symbols in enhancing the spiritual quality of their environment, by

placing items that hold personal spiritual significance—religious icons, nature elements, or art that inspires transcendence—the seeker turns their space into a living altar, a constant reminder of the divine presence.

In the quest for harmony, the voyager explores the principles of sacred geometry and fend shui, understanding how the arrangement and orientation of space can influence energy flow and spiritual resonance. This mindful approach to spatial design aligns the seeker's environment with cosmic order and beneficial energies.

The traveler learns that cultivating plants and the presence of natural elements indoors can greatly enhance the vibrancy and harmony of their living spaces. The inclusion of greenery not only purifies the air but also brings the calming and grounding energies of nature into daily life, supporting the seeker's connection to the Earth.

Through their journey, the nomad realizes the importance of reducing clutter and material excess in creating peaceful environments. Simplifying one's space and possessions not only clears physical clutter but also mental and emotional clutter, fostering clarity, focus, and serenity.

The adept finds that the practice of blessing and expressing gratitude for their space deepens the spiritual connection with their environment. Regularly acknowledging the sanctuary that supports their journey amplifies its sacredness, turning it into a true refuge of peace and spiritual nourishment.

In cultivating harmony in the environment, the sojourner becomes acutely aware of the impact of their ecological footprint. They strive to make sustainable and ethical choices, recognizing that caring for the planet is an extension of their spiritual values and a contribution to global harmony.

Finally, the seeker understands that cultivating peace and harmony in their environment is a dynamic and ongoing act of co-creation with the divine. By infusing their surroundings with intention, care, and reverence, the seeker not only enhances their own spiritual path but also contributes to the elevation of collective consciousness, creating ripples of harmony that extend far beyond their immediate environment. Through this mindful stewardship, the seeker embodies the principle that outer peace begins with inner peace, and in nurturing the sanctity of their surroundings, they honor the sacredness of all life.

Chapter 10

In the advanced stages of the spiritual journey, the seeker is called to embody the spiritual principles they have internalized, bringing the essence of their inner transformation into the realm of daily life. This exploration reveals how the seeker can become a living testament to spiritual values, influencing their environment and interactions through the vibrancy of their being.

The adept learns that embodying spiritual principles begins with a commitment to live authentically, aligning thoughts, words, and actions with their highest truths. This authenticity becomes a beacon of integrity and sincerity, inspiring trust and respect in those around them.

As the wayfarer integrates spiritual values into their behavior, they prioritize kindness, compassion, and empathy in their interactions. These virtues, expressed in even the smallest acts, contribute to a culture of understanding and benevolence, counteracting the tendencies toward indifference and disconnect prevalent in society.

The pilgrim discovers the importance of mindfulness in embodying spiritual principles. By remaining present and aware, the seeker ensures that their responses to life's challenges are thoughtful and considered, reflecting their spiritual commitments rather than reactive patterns.

In the quest to manifest spiritual insights outwardly, the voyager embraces the practice of non-judgment. Recognizing the divine spark in all beings, the seeker transcends superficial differences, fostering an environment of acceptance and unity.

The traveler learns that embodying spiritual principles involves courageous action. Whether standing up for justice, engaging in acts of service, or advocating for peace, the seeker actively participates in the creation of a more compassionate and equitable world, grounded in their spiritual convictions.

Through their journey, the nomad realizes that consistency is key to embodying spiritual principles. They strive to maintain their spiritual commitments in all circumstances, understanding that it is the accumulation of countless conscious choices that shapes their character and influence.

The adept finds that patience and perseverance are essential virtues in manifesting spiritual principles. The path of embodiment is marked by challenges and setbacks, but the seeker remains steadfast, trusting in the transformative power of sustained spiritual practice.

In their exploration, the sojourner discovers the joy of collective spirituality. By connecting with like-minded individuals and communities, the seeker amplifies their impact, collaborating on initiatives that reflect their shared values and vision for a better world.

Finally, the seeker understands that embodying spiritual principles in daily life is an ongoing process of growth and refinement. Each day presents new opportunities to express their spiritual insights in tangible ways, contributing to personal evolution and the collective upliftment of humanity. Through this dedicated practice, the seeker not only transforms their own life but also becomes a conduit for positive change in the world, embodying the true essence of spiritual living.

In the conscious journey towards a harmonious existence, the seeker embraces sustainable living not merely as an ecological responsibility but as a profound spiritual practice. This exploration delves into how living in alignment with Earth's rhythms and resources reflects a deep respect for the interconnected web of life, embodying the spiritual principles of stewardship, gratitude, and reverence for all forms of existence.

The adept discovers that sustainable living begins with a shift in perspective, seeing the Earth as a sacred entity, a living being with which they have a reciprocal relationship. This realization fosters a sense of deep connection and responsibility, guiding the seeker to make choices that honor and preserve the planet's vitality and diversity.

As the wayfarer adopts practices of sustainability, they learn the art of mindful consumption, choosing to support products and processes that are kind to the Earth and its inhabitants. This mindful approach extends to all aspects of living, from food and energy to transportation and waste, reflecting a commitment to minimizing harm and promoting ecological balance.

The pilgrim finds that simplicity and minimalism are key tenets of sustainable living. By reducing material possessions and unnecessary complexities, the seeker not only lessens their environmental impact but also cultivates inner peace and contentment, discovering the richness of a life defined by quality, not quantity.

In the realm of food, the voyager explores the spiritual dimensions of eating, recognizing the act of nourishment as a sacred exchange between themselves and the Earth. They gravitate towards locally sourced, organic, and plant-based foods, acknowledging the energy and life force in what they consume and its effect on their spiritual and physical well-being.

The traveler learns that sustainable living involves active participation in the healing of the planet. Whether through reforestation efforts, community clean-ups, or advocating for environmental policies, the seeker understands that their actions contribute to a collective effort to restore balance and harmony to the natural world.

Through their commitment to sustainability, the nomad discovers the power of creativity and innovation. They explore alternative energies, sustainable technologies, and green initiatives, seeing these advancements as expressions of human ingenuity in service to the Earth and future generations.

The adept finds that teaching and sharing knowledge on sustainability is a vital aspect of their spiritual practice. By educating others on the importance of ecological stewardship, the seeker spreads awareness and inspires change, amplifying their impact beyond individual actions.

In their journey, the sojourner learns that sustainable living is a path of continuous learning and adaptation. They remain open to new information, willing to adjust their habits and practices as they discover more effective ways to live in harmony with the planet.

Finally, the seeker realizes that sustainable living as a spiritual practice is a profound act of love—love for the Earth, for its myriad creatures, and for the human community. By choosing to live sustainably, the seeker affirms their interconnectedness with all life, embodying the principles of compassion, respect, and unity that lie at the heart of spiritual growth. Through this dedicated practice, the seeker not only contributes to the well-being of the planet but also deepens their own spiritual journey, living as a testament to the sacred bond between humanity and the Earth.

In the journey of spiritual maturity, the seeker recognizes activism not merely as a call to social and political engagement but as a profound form of spiritual service. This exploration delves into how advocating for justice, equality, and the preservation of the planet reflects the highest ideals of compassion, interconnectedness, and love in action.

The adept learns that spiritual activism is grounded in the recognition of the inherent worth and dignity of all beings. Inspired by this understanding, the seeker becomes a voice for the voiceless and a defender of the rights and freedoms of all life forms, human and non-human alike.

As the wayfarer engages in acts of activism, they discover the importance of operating from a place of centeredness and peace. By anchoring their actions in spiritual principles, the seeker ensures that their advocacy is not driven by anger or divisiveness but by a genuine desire for healing and unity.

The pilgrim finds that compassion is the heart of spiritual activism. This compassion extends beyond empathy to include practical actions aimed at alleviating suffering and creating a more just and compassionate world. Through their efforts, the seeker embodies the belief that change begins with the transformation of the individual heart and ripples outward.

In the realm of spiritual activism, the voyager learns to balance action with contemplation. They understand that to be effective in their advocacy, they must also cultivate inner resilience and wisdom, drawing on their spiritual practices to replenish their energy and maintain their commitment to the cause.

The traveler discovers that spiritual activism embraces a holistic approach, recognizing the interconnectedness of all issues. Whether addressing climate change, social inequality, or any form of injustice, the seeker sees these challenges as interwoven threads of a larger tapestry, requiring a comprehensive and integrated response.

Through their commitment to activism, the nomad realizes the power of collective action. By joining forces with like-minded individuals and groups, the seeker amplifies their impact, creating a synergistic effect that can bring about significant social and environmental change.

The adept finds that spiritual activism involves continuous learning and openness to different perspectives. By staying informed and listening to the experiences of those directly affected by injustice, the seeker deepens their understanding and effectiveness as an advocate for change.

In their journey, the sojourner experiences the transformative potential of activism to inspire spiritual growth. Through the challenges and triumphs of advocacy, the seeker develops qualities such as courage, perseverance, and a deep sense of purpose, further enriching their spiritual path.

Finally, the seeker understands that activism as a form of spiritual service is a powerful expression of their highest values and an integral aspect of their spiritual identity. By dedicating themselves to the betterment of the world, the seeker not only contributes to tangible change but also aligns their actions with the cosmic principles of love, justice, and unity. Through this sacred commitment, the seeker becomes a beacon of hope and a catalyst for positive transformation, embodying the essence of spiritual activism.

In the evolving journey of spiritual integration, the seeker comes to recognize the profound significance of community and the collective consciousness in amplifying spiritual insights and fostering global transformation. This exploration highlights how the collective—formed by individuals united in spirit and purpose—becomes a powerful vessel for the expression of universal love, wisdom, and healing.

The adept learns that community offers a mirror to the self, reflecting both the beauty and areas for growth within each individual. By engaging in spiritual communities, the seeker is provided with opportunities for learning, sharing, and growth that are magnified in the presence of others walking similar paths.

As the wayfarer delves into the concept of collective consciousness, they discover that every thought, emotion, and action contributes to this shared energetic field. The seeker becomes more mindful of their contributions to the collective, striving to infuse it with positivity, compassion, and light.

The pilgrim finds that spiritual communities serve as sanctuaries of support and encouragement. In times of doubt or challenge, the community acts as a haven, offering guidance, understanding, and the strength found in shared experience and collective intention.

In the realm of collective consciousness, the voyager learns the transformative power of group meditation and prayer. When individuals come together with a unified purpose, their spiritual efforts are exponentially magnified, creating ripples of healing, peace, and consciousness expansion that extend far beyond the immediate environment.

The traveler discovers that community engagement and service are natural extensions of spiritual practice. By contributing to the welfare of their community, the seeker practices living expressions of spiritual principles, weaving the values of altruism, kindness, and unity into the fabric of everyday life.

Through their engagement with community, the nomad realizes the diversity within unity. Spiritual communities thrive on the unique contributions of each member, celebrating differences as strengths that enrich the collective journey towards enlightenment and understanding.

The adept finds that fostering community and nurturing collective consciousness require active participation and commitment. By taking on roles of leadership, mentorship, or support, the seeker contributes to the vitality and growth of their spiritual community, ensuring it remains a vibrant source of collective wisdom and inspiration.

In their journey, the sojourner experiences the joy and fulfillment that come from contributing to a collective vision. Working alongside others towards a shared goal—be it environmental stewardship, social justice, or spiritual awakening—the seeker finds a deeper sense of purpose and connection.

Finally, the seeker understands that the cultivation of community and the elevation of collective consciousness are essential to the spiritual evolution of humanity. By valuing and actively participating in these communal spaces, the seeker not only accelerates their own growth but also contributes to the awakening of the planet. Through the power of community and collective intention, the seeker helps to manifest a world rooted in harmony, compassion, and spiritual unity, embodying the true potential of collective consciousness in action.

In the contemporary landscape of spiritual exploration, the seeker recognizes the potential of technology as a tool for enhancing spiritual growth and fostering connections within the global spiritual community. This journey explores how digital platforms, online resources, and modern communication tools can be mindfully utilized to support the seeker's path and to spread spiritual awareness across the globe.

The adept learns that technology, when used with intention and discernment, can significantly expand access to spiritual teachings and practices. Online courses, webinars, and virtual retreats offer opportunities for learning and engagement that transcend geographical limitations, allowing seekers worldwide to tap into wisdom traditions from the comfort of their homes.

As the wayfarer navigates the digital realm, they discover online communities and forums that serve as virtual sanctuaries for sharing insights, experiences, and support. These platforms foster a sense of belonging and connection among individuals who, despite physical distances, share a common spiritual journey.

The pilgrim finds that technology can be a powerful medium for meditation and mindfulness practices. Apps and online programs offering guided meditations, mindfulness exercises, and spiritual music provide accessible tools for maintaining a consistent practice amidst the demands of modern life.

In the exploration of technology's role in spiritual growth, the voyager learns the importance of balance and mindful consumption. They become adept at discerning the quality and vibrational impact of digital content, choosing resources that uplift and inspire rather than distract or deplete their energy.

The traveler discovers the transformative potential of using technology for altruistic and spiritual purposes. Crowdfunding platforms, social media campaigns, and online petitions become avenues for mobilizing collective action for causes aligned with spiritual values, demonstrating the power of technology to effect positive change in the world.

Through their engagement with digital tools, the nomad realizes the value of digital detoxes and technology sabbaths. Periodically disconnecting from digital devices and platforms becomes a practice of presence and reconnection with the inner self and the natural world, highlighting the need for balance in the digital age.

The adept finds that technology offers unique ways to document and share their spiritual journey. Blogs, vlogs, and social media platforms become outlets for expressing insights, challenges, and breakthroughs, inspiring others on their path and contributing to the collective tapestry of spiritual exploration.

In their journey, the sojourner witnesses the emergence of spiritually oriented technologies that blend ancient wisdom with modern innovation. Virtual reality meditations, biofeedback devices for mindfulness training, and apps that track spiritual practices illustrate the evolving landscape of technology-assisted spiritual development.

Finally, the seeker understands that harnessing technology for spiritual growth and connection is a reflection of the evolving nature of the spiritual path itself. By integrating technology mindfully and purposefully into their practice, the seeker not only enhances their own development but also contributes to the creation of an interconnected, spiritually aware global community. Through this mindful integration, technology becomes a bridge, linking hearts and minds in the shared pursuit of awakening and transformation.

In the journey toward holistic spiritual actualization, the seeker delves into the practice of ethical living as the manifestation of spiritual integrity. This path illuminates the inseparable link between one's values and daily actions, emphasizing how ethical conduct in personal, professional, and societal realms serves as a testament to the depth of one's spiritual convictions.

The adept recognizes that ethical living begins with self-reflection and an honest assessment of how their choices and behaviors align with their spiritual principles. This introspection leads to a commitment to act with honesty, compassion, and fairness, ensuring that their interactions reflect their highest ethical standards.

As the wayfarer cultivates a life of integrity, they understand the importance of consistency in words and deeds. The seeker strives to be a living embodiment of their spiritual beliefs, understanding that true integrity means that their actions are congruent with their values, even when no one is watching.

The pilgrim explores the concept of ahimsa, or non-harm, as a foundational ethical principle. By adopting practices that minimize harm to all living beings and the planet, the seeker fosters a deep respect for life in all its forms, embodying the interconnectedness at the heart of their spiritual worldview.

In the realm of ethical living, the voyager learns the value of conscious consumption. They make mindful choices about the food they eat, the products they buy, and the companies they support, aiming to contribute to a sustainable and just economy that honors the dignity of all beings and the health of the Earth.

The traveler discovers that spiritual integrity involves active engagement with the world's challenges. Whether advocating for social justice, environmental stewardship, or human rights, the seeker views activism as an expression of their spiritual commitment to healing, justice, and unity.

Through their commitment to ethical living, the nomad realizes the power of example. By embodying ethical principles in their daily life, the seeker becomes a beacon of inspiration and a catalyst for positive change, encouraging others to consider the impact of their own choices and actions.

The adept finds that ethical dilemmas and challenges offer opportunities for growth and deepening of spiritual understanding. Facing these situations with courage, humility, and a willingness to learn, the seeker strengthens their ethical compass and refines their ability to navigate complex moral landscapes.

In their journey, the sojourner embraces forgiveness and compassion as essential aspects of ethical living. Recognizing their own imperfections and those of others, the seeker cultivates an attitude of understanding and grace, fostering an environment where growth and reconciliation are possible.

Finally, the seeker understands that ethical living and spiritual integrity are not static achievements but dynamic practices that evolve over a lifetime. By continually striving to live in alignment with their spiritual values, the seeker not only enhances their own spiritual journey but also contributes to the collective upliftment of humanity. Through the practice of ethical living, the seeker affirms that spirituality is not confined to moments of contemplation or ritual but is woven into the very fabric of daily existence, manifesting as actions that honor the sacredness of life and the interconnected web of existence.

In the deepening journey of spiritual unfoldment, the seeker recognizes the invaluable role of mentorship and guidance not only in their own path but also in the broader spiritual ecosystem. This exploration delves into the art of spiritual mentorship, highlighting how sharing wisdom, experiences, and support serves as a vital conduit for collective growth and enlightenment.

The adept discovers that true spiritual mentorship is rooted in humility and the recognition that guidance is a mutual journey of discovery. The mentor and mentee walk together, learning from each other, with the mentor facilitating rather than dictating the path, embodying the principle that every soul is unique and each journey is personal.

As the wayfarer steps into the role of mentor, they realize the importance of active listening and presence. By fully attending to the individual before them, the mentor honors the mentee's experiences and aspirations, providing a safe and nurturing space for exploration and growth.

The pilgrim finds that effective spiritual mentorship involves leading by example. The mentor embodies the values, practices, and attitudes they advocate, inspiring through their own commitment to the path and demonstrating the transformative power of living in alignment with spiritual principles.

In the realm of guidance, the voyager learns the significance of intuition and discernment. The mentor uses these tools to sense the mentee's needs, offering insights and advice that resonate with the mentee's current state and potential for growth, avoiding a one-size-fits-all approach to spiritual development.

The traveler discovers that mentorship extends beyond the transmission of knowledge to include the sharing of energy and intention. Through their presence and focused attention, the mentor amplifies the mentee's capacity for self-realization, acting as a catalyst for the mentee's spiritual awakening and empowerment.

Through their engagement in mentorship, the nomad recognizes the value of vulnerability and openness. By sharing their own challenges, doubts, and breakthroughs, the mentor demystifies the spiritual journey, encouraging the mentee to embrace their path with all its ups and downs.

The adept finds that spiritual mentorship is a dynamic and evolving relationship. As the mentee grows, the nature of the mentorship may shift, reflecting the deepening understanding and changing needs of both parties, and underscoring the journey's cyclical and fluid nature.

In their journey, the sojourner appreciates the broader impact of mentorship on the spiritual community. By fostering individual growth, mentorship strengthens the collective fabric of spiritual seekers, creating a supportive network of wisdom, compassion, and shared purpose.

Finally, the seeker understands that engaging in spiritual mentorship and guidance is both a privilege and a responsibility. It is an opportunity to serve the greater good, to pass on the light of wisdom, and to contribute to the ongoing cycle of learning and awakening. By offering mentorship, the seeker not only aids in the growth of others but also deepens their own understanding and connection to the divine, affirming that in the act of giving, both mentor and mentee receive, and the sacred flow of spiritual lineage is preserved and enriched for future generations.

In the sacred journey towards deeper spiritual understanding, the seeker comes to embrace the concept of spiritual ecology, recognizing the profound connection between their inner spiritual life and the health of the planet. This exploration delves into living in harmony with the Earth, acknowledging it as a living entity and understanding that environmental stewardship is a critical aspect of spiritual practice.

The adept learns that spiritual ecology is grounded in the recognition of the Earth as a sacred creation, imbued with divine presence. This perspective fosters a deep reverence for all forms of life and the ecosystems that sustain them, guiding the seeker to engage with the natural world with respect, gratitude, and care.

As the wayfarer deepens their connection with the Earth, they discover the interconnectedness of all living beings. This awareness of oneness with the planet shifts the seeker's actions towards sustainability, conservation, and regeneration, aligning their lifestyle with principles that support the Earth's well-being.

The pilgrim finds that practices such as spending time in nature, engaging in earth-based rituals, and celebrating seasonal cycles enhance their spiritual connection and ecological awareness. These practices remind the seeker of the natural rhythms and cycles that govern life, inviting them to live in sync with these patterns.

In the realm of spiritual ecology, the voyager learns the importance of mindful consumption. They become conscious of the impact of their choices on the environment, opting for lifestyles and products that minimize harm to the planet and promote sustainability, reflecting their commitment to the Earth's health.

The traveler discovers that activism and advocacy for environmental causes are natural extensions of spiritual ecology. By standing up for the protection of natural habitats, biodiversity, and the rights of indigenous peoples, the seeker puts their spiritual values into action, contributing to the healing of the planet.

Through their engagement with spiritual ecology, the nomad realizes the transformative power of community in effecting environmental change. Joining or forming communities focused on ecological stewardship amplifies the impact of their efforts, creating a collective force for positive change in harmony with spiritual principles.

The adept finds that teaching and sharing knowledge about spiritual ecology is crucial. By educating others about the spiritual significance of living in harmony with the Earth, the seeker spreads awareness and inspires a broader cultural shift towards ecological consciousness and reverence for life.

In their journey, the sojourner learns to see challenges to the Earth's health not only as environmental issues but also as spiritual crises. This understanding motivates the seeker to integrate ecological healing into their spiritual practice, recognizing that the health of the planet is intrinsically linked to the collective spiritual evolution of humanity.

Finally, the seeker understands that spiritual ecology is an ongoing commitment to live in a way that honors the sacredness of the Earth and all its inhabitants. By embracing this path, the seeker not only deepens their spiritual awareness but also becomes an active participant in the creation of a more harmonious, sustainable, and spiritually attuned world. Through the practice of spiritual ecology, the seeker embodies the principle that to heal the Earth is to heal oneself, and to honor the Earth is to honor the divine.

In the continuous journey of spiritual enrichment, the seeker recognizes the transformative power of creating and nurturing spaces dedicated to spiritual reflection and community gathering. This exploration delves into the importance of physical and virtual environments that facilitate inner growth, collective worship, and the shared pursuit of spiritual understanding.

The adept learns that spaces for spiritual reflection—be it sanctuaries, meditation rooms, or natural settings—are vital for deepening one's connection to the divine. These sacred spaces provide a respite from the hustle and bustle of daily life, offering the tranquility and focus necessary for profound contemplation and spiritual practice.

As the wayfarer embarks on creating these spaces, they discover the significance of intentionality in their design and use. Elements such as natural light, serene colors, symbolic decorations, and the presence of nature are carefully chosen to enhance the spiritual ambiance and foster a sense of peace and sanctity.

The pilgrim finds that community gathering spaces play a crucial role in spiritual life, serving as hubs for learning, sharing, and connection. Whether through organized events, group meditations, or communal rituals, these spaces encourage the formation of spiritual bonds and the collective exploration of existential truths.

In the realm of digital connectivity, the voyager learns to harness online platforms to create virtual spaces for spiritual engagement. Websites, social media groups, and online forums become accessible venues for seekers worldwide to connect, share insights, and support each other's growth, transcending geographical limitations.

The traveler discovers the power of inclusivity in fostering vibrant spiritual communities. By welcoming individuals from diverse backgrounds, beliefs, and experiences, the seeker enriches the communal tapestry, facilitating a rich exchange of perspectives and deepening the collective understanding of spirituality.

Through their engagement in creating and nurturing these spaces, the nomad realizes the importance of ongoing care and evolution. Just as the spiritual journey is dynamic, so too are the spaces that support it, requiring regular reevaluation and adaptation to meet the changing needs of the community.

The adept finds that leadership and stewardship are key to sustaining spiritual spaces and communities. By stepping into roles of responsibility, the seeker ensures that these sanctuaries remain places of respect, growth, and harmony, guided by principles of love, service, and spiritual integrity.

In their journey, the sojourner learns that creating spaces for spiritual reflection and community extends beyond physical or virtual environments. It involves cultivating an inner space of openness and receptivity, allowing the seeker to carry the essence of sanctuary within them, wherever they go.

Finally, the seeker understands that fostering spaces for spiritual reflection and community is a profound service to the world. By contributing to the creation and maintenance of these sacred spaces, the seeker not only supports their own spiritual journey but also facilitates the spiritual awakening and interconnectedness of the broader human family. Through this dedicated effort, the seeker helps to weave a global network of sanctuaries, each a beacon of light and a testament to the collective yearning for deeper meaning, unity, and peace.

In the culminating exploration of Chapter 10, the seeker turns their attention towards the concept of global spirituality—a unifying vision that transcends individual beliefs and practices to embrace a collective commitment to planetary healing and consciousness evolution. This journey illuminates how spiritual interconnectedness can foster a world characterized by peace, sustainability, and universal compassion.

The adept recognizes that global spirituality is not about erasing diverse spiritual traditions but rather celebrating and weaving together these rich tapestries to form a holistic vision of healing for the Earth and all its inhabitants. It is an acknowledgment that at the core of all spiritual paths lies a common thread of love, reverence for life, and a recognition of our interconnected fate.

As the wayfarer engages with the principles of global spirituality, they understand the importance of empathy and solidarity across cultural, religious, and geographical divides. This empathy becomes a powerful force for bridging gaps and building a global community united in the purpose of healing and elevating the collective consciousness.

The pilgrim finds that global spirituality calls for an active engagement with the world's challenges, from environmental degradation to social injustices. It inspires a spirituality that is not confined to personal enlightenment but extends to active participation in creating solutions that benefit the planet and future generations.

In the realm of global spirituality, the voyager learns the significance of collective rituals and ceremonies that honor the Earth and human unity. Whether through global meditation events, interfaith gatherings, or celebrations of the natural world, these shared practices strengthen the bonds between diverse spiritual communities and amplify intentions for healing and peace.

The traveler discovers that technology and digital connectivity play crucial roles in fostering global spirituality. Through these tools, seekers worldwide can share wisdom, support each other's growth, and mobilize for causes that reflect their shared spiritual values, creating a virtual yet tangible network of light and consciousness.

Through their commitment to global spirituality, the nomad realizes the transformative potential of envisioning a better world. By holding a collective vision of peace, sustainability, and harmony, the spiritual community contributes to the manifestation of these ideals, leveraging the power of focused intention and prayer.

The adept finds that educating and inspiring the younger generations about the principles of global spirituality is essential for its perpetuation. By instilling values of compassion, stewardship, and unity from an early age, the seeker helps to cultivate a future leadership rooted in spiritual wisdom and planetary consciousness.

In their journey, the sojourner embraces the realization that global spirituality is an ever-evolving process, reflective of humanity's growing understanding of its place in the cosmos and its responsibility to the web of life. It is a dynamic invitation to contribute to a living tapestry of spiritual unity and action.

Finally, the seeker understands that embracing global spirituality for planetary healing is the ultimate expression of spiritual maturity. It signifies a shift from individual awakening to collective transformation, embodying the belief that our shared destiny is intricately linked and that together, united in spirit and purpose, we can forge a path towards a healed, harmonious, and spiritually awakened world. Through this expansive embrace, the seeker not only contributes to the current tapestry of global spirituality but also lays the foundations for a legacy of love, wisdom, and unity for generations to come.

conclusion:

In this profound exploration of spirituality and its application in the modern world, we've journeyed through the depths of individual awakening to the heights of collective consciousness, uncovering the vast landscapes of inner growth, communal harmony, and global healing. This book serves as a testament to the seeker's path, offering a rich tapestry of insights, practices, and philosophies that guide the soul toward enlightenment and beyond.

At the heart of our exploration lies the understanding that spirituality is not a destination but a journey—a continuous unfolding of awareness, understanding, and connection. We've seen how the quest for personal transformation is deeply interwoven with the fabric of daily life, where mundane activities become sacred rituals, and every interaction carries the potential for profound spiritual growth.

We delved into the art of mindfulness, conscious communication, and the cultivation of virtues such as compassion, empathy, and integrity. These practices emerged as foundational stones, building a life of authenticity and purpose. Through the lens of spiritual ecology, we embraced the Earth as a sacred entity, recognizing our role as stewards of its health and harmony, and acknowledging that our spiritual well-being is inextricably linked to the planet's vitality.

The exploration of global spirituality illuminated the power of diversity within unity, showing us that the merging of various spiritual traditions can forge a holistic vision for planetary healing. We learned that spiritual communities, both physical and virtual, serve as havens of support and growth, emphasizing the importance of collective efforts in the elevation of consciousness.

Technology, when used mindfully, was revealed as a valuable ally in the spiritual journey, extending the reach of ancient wisdom and fostering connections across the globe. This digital age offers unprecedented opportunities for sharing, learning, and uniting in spiritual purpose, underscoring the evolving nature of how we seek and spread enlightenment.

Ethical living emerged as a concrete expression of spiritual integrity, highlighting the alignment of actions with spiritual values as essential for authentic existence. Through ethical choices, we not only navigate our personal paths with clarity and honor but also contribute to the betterment of the wider community and world.

The book emphasized the significance of mentorship and guidance in spiritual growth, illustrating how the sharing of wisdom and experiences enriches both the mentor and mentee, knitting tighter the fabric of the spiritual community. This dynamic exchange fosters a lineage of enlightenment that transcends time and space, nurturing the seeds of wisdom in generations to come.

We explored the concept of spiritual ecology, advocating for a lifestyle that honors our deep connection with the natural world. This holistic approach to living underscores the unity of all existence and our responsibility towards the Earth, advocating for practices that promote its health and our spiritual fulfillment.

The creation of spaces for spiritual reflection and community gatherings was highlighted as essential for nurturing the soul and fostering bonds among seekers. These sacred spaces, both physical and virtual, offer solace, inspiration, and connection, serving as wellsprings of spiritual vitality and communal support.

In conclusion, this book serves as a beacon for all seekers on the path, illuminating the myriad ways in which spirituality can be woven into the fabric of everyday life. It calls upon each reader to embark on their unique journey of discovery, transformation, and service, encouraging a life lived in deep connection with the self, the community, and the planet. Through the practices, insights, and philosophies shared within these pages, we are invited to co-create a world of harmony, understanding, and awakened consciousness—a testament to the indomitable spirit of humanity and the boundless possibilities of the spiritual path.

complete list of references

Creating a list of references that delve into spiritual qualities and evolution offers a treasure trove of wisdom for those on the path of personal and collective spiritual growth. Below is a curated selection of books that span a range of perspectives, traditions, and insights into the spiritual journey:

"The Power of Now: A Guide to Spiritual Enlightenment" by Eckhart Tolle - This book has become a modern classic, emphasizing the importance of living in the present moment and transcending the ego for spiritual awakening.

"A New Earth: Awakening to Your Life's Purpose" by Eckhart Tolle - Tolle expands on his teachings by exploring how a shift in consciousness can lead to personal and global transformation.

"The Book of Awakening: Having the Life You Want by Being Present to the Life You Have" by Mark Nepo - A daily companion offering spiritual insights and practical wisdom to connect with our true selves and the world around us.

"The Untethered Soul: The Journey Beyond Yourself" by Michael A. Singer - Singer presents a straightforward and transformative exploration of self-identity, freedom, and the path to spiritual liberation.

"Autobiography of a Yogi" by Paramahansa Yogananda - This classic introduces readers to the life of Paramahansa Yogananda and his encounters with spiritual figures, offering insights into the science and philosophy of yoga and meditation.

"The Seat of the Soul" by Gary Zukav - Zukav explores the alignment of the personality with the soul as the foundation for spiritual growth and the evolution of consciousness.

"Anatomy of the Spirit: The Seven Stages of Power and Healing" by Caroline Myss - This book offers a unique blend of spiritual and psychological wisdom, exploring the connection between spiritual health and physical well-being.

"The Four Agreements: A Practical Guide to Personal Freedom" by Don Miguel Ruiz - Ruiz presents a simple yet profound code of personal conduct learned from Toltec wisdom that can rapidly transform our lives to a new experience of freedom, true happiness, and love.

"Braiding Sweetgrass: Indigenous Wisdom, Scientific Knowledge, and the Teachings of Plants" by Robin Wall Kimmerer - Blending science, spirituality, and traditional indigenous knowledge, Kimmerer invites readers to consider the deep connection between humanity and the natural world.

"Living Buddha, Living Christ" by Thich Nhat Hanh - Through this book, the renowned Zen master illustrates the interconnectedness of the core beliefs of Christianity and Buddhism, offering a unifying perspective on spirituality and practice.

"The Essential Rumi, Translated by Coleman Barks - A collection of poems by Rumi, the 13th-century Persian poet, theologian, and Sufi mystic, which continues to inspire millions worldwide with its insights into love, spirituality, and the nature of existence.

"Falling into Grace: Insights on the End of Suffering" by Adyashanti - Adyashanti invites readers on a journey to discover the truth beyond the bounds of the ego and to experience the peace and freedom that come with falling into grace.

Each of these works provides unique insights into the pursuit of spiritual qualities, the journey of evolution, and the embodiment of spiritual principles in everyday life. They serve as valuable companions for anyone seeking to deepen their understanding and experience of the spiritual path.

Cru (www.cru.org) - Offers a wide range of articles and resources focused on spiritual growth, including how to grow spiritually, trust God in difficult times, and integrate God-centered prayer into daily life.

Butterfly Living (butterflyliving.org) - Presents keys to spiritual growth and a closer walk with God, offering insights into developing a deeper spiritual life through intentional practice and connection with the divine.

Ligonier Ministries (www.ligonier.org) - Provides comprehensive resources on spiritual growth from a Christian perspective, emphasizing the continuous nature of spiritual development from conversion through to maturity.

Desiring God (www.desiringgod.org) - Focuses on the importance of spiritual growth not being accidental and the role of intentional spiritual practice in cultivating a deeper relationship with God.

Please enjoy your travels and evolutions in all its forms and capacities.

Be well always,

Dr. Victor Denis Purcell

Cru (www.cru.org) - Offers a wide range of articles and resources focused on spiritual growth, including how to grow spiritually, trust God in difficult times, and integrate God-centered prayer into daily life.

Butterfly Living (butterflyliving.org) - Presents keys to spiritual growth and a closer walk with God, offering insights into developing a deeper spiritual life through intentional practice and connection with the divine.

Ligonier Ministries (www.ligonier.org) - Provides comprehensive resources on spiritual growth from a Christian perspective, emphasizing the continuous nature of spiritual development from conversion through to maturity.

Desiring God (www.desiringgod.org) –

Focuses on the importance of spiritual growth not being accidental and the role of intentional spiritual practice in cultivating a deeper relationship with God.